D0982783

MIDDLE EASTERN
Political Systems

MIDDLE EASTERN
Political Systems

DANKWART A. RUSTOW
The City University of New York

Prentice-Hall, Inc., Englewood Cliffs, New Jersey

COMPARATIVE ASIAN GOVERNMENTS SERIES

Editors
ROBERT E. WARD
ROY C. MACRIDIS

Much of the material in this book
appeared originally in
Modern Political Systems: Asia,
edited by
Robert E. Ward and Roy C. Macridis.

Current printing (last digit):
10 9 8 7 6 5 4 3 2 1

P–13–581587–8
C–13–581595–9

Library of Congress Catalog Card No.
75–126829

320.956
R971

Printed in the United States of America

PRENTICE-HALL INTERNATIONAL, INC., *London*
PRENTICE-HALL OF AUSTRALIA PTY. LTD., *Sydney*
PRENTICE-HALL OF CANADA, LTD., *Toronto*
PRENTICE-HALL OF INDIA PRIVATE LIMITED, *New Delhi*
PRENTICE-HALL OF JAPAN, INC., *Tokyo*

FOREWORD

This series is dedicated to the proposition that it is no longer valid or profitable to study comparative politics within an essentially North American- and European-centered frame of reference. Although admittedly more familiar, more comprehensible, and—in the past, at least—closer and more important to us, the political histories, ideologies, and institutions of these areas constitute only a small (though vital) fragment of the political universe with which the student of contemporary political systems must be concerned. Politically speaking, the history of the twentieth century is in large part the history of the re-emergence of non-European areas and states to positions of independence and prominence on the world scene. We can ignore this fact only at our peril.

Asia, Latin America, and Africa together account for approximately sixty-three per cent of the land area and seventy-five per cent of the population of the earth. Today, three factors combine to give new meaning and importance to these figures. First, the age of imperialism and colonialism—at least in the classic sense of these terms—has been largely liquidated. Thus non-Western states—often themselves but recent graduates from colonial status—are obtaining a degree of political independence and freedom of decision and maneuver which is, in a collective sense, unique in their recent histories.

Second, this development is both impelled and accompanied by what is often referred to as "a revolution of rising expectations." Great masses of people in the underdeveloped areas are being exposed to the highly revolutionary concept that meaningful types of economic, political, and social change are possible in their countries, and that these carry with them the promise of a better

life for themselves and their children. They are becoming actively dissatisfied
with the products and performance of their traditional societies and in increasing numbers are demanding some measure of modernization. It happens that
these demands coincide with a period when the skills and technologies necessary to support such modernization are for the first time becoming widely
available. Thus most of the governments of these non-Western states—some
eagerly, others with trepidation and reluctance—are being committed to more
or less systematic long-term efforts to modernize at least segments of their
societies. Gradually, therefore, the technological and power gap which has long
separated West from non-West is beginning to narrow, and the material circumstances of the two areas are becoming less disparate.

Third, both of the previously mentioned developments are taking place at a
time when modern communications and weaponry have made all men uneasy
neighbors in a world where global rivalries and ceaseless competition between
the "democratic" and "Communist" approaches to political, economic, and social
problems have become predominant international problems. In such circumstances, the political and military weakness of most of these non-Western states
is no longer so controlling a factor. In the first place, this weakness is not a fixed
condition; some of these states, such as China, have become formidable powers
in their own right. In the second place, the very existence of the present international tensions endows them with an importance and with possibilities of maneuver which they might otherwise lack. No matter how remote their location or
"underdeveloped" their circumstances, the territory, resources, skills, and alle-
giances of each of these states are of significant value in this struggle. From this
complex of factors is emerging a world which—even in the conduct of its
hostilities—is characterized by new degrees and dimensions of unity and inter-
dependence.

It is essential that the discipline of comparative politics keep abreast of such
developments and expand its frames of reference and concern to include the
political systems of these emergent non-Western areas. Such a resolution is
easy to make, but hard to put into practice. The governments involved are so
numerous, their political heritages and institutions so complex and diverse, and
the materials and skills relevant to their study and analysis so scattered, uneven in quality, and difficult to use that—for introductory purposes, anyway—
we must be highly selective. In the present volume, we direct attention only
to the political systems of the Middle East; other books in this series deal in comparable terms with the Chinese People's Republic, India, Southeast Asia, and
Japan. A further volume treats the political systems of England, France, West
Germany, and the U.S.S.R. All were designed in accordance with certain shared
views about the nature of modern political systems and the manner in which
these may most meaningfully be compared. To make clear the nature of these
shared views, we may begin by stating what we believe a political system to be
and what factors we hold to be relevant to the comparison of political systems.
This will involve the identification of those qualities and problems which we will
treat in the case of the Middle East and of the political systems under consideration in other volumes of the series.

A political system is a mechanism for the identification and posing of problems and the making and administering of decisions in the realm of public

affairs, an area which is variously defined by different societies. The official machinery by which these problems and decisions are legally identified, posed, made, and administered is called government. Government provides both an official, authoritative mechanism for the identification and posing of problems and the making and administering of decisions and a means of formalizing and bestowing legitimacy on the products of this process. In practice, it does more than this; by providing a context and an apparatus for the making of official decisions, it also comes to influence the types of problems which are posed and decisions which are taken.

Government—in the sense of society's legislative, executive, judicial, and bureaucratic machinery—is not, however, the sole concern of students of comparative politics; for it is only a part of the political system as a whole, which includes, in addition to government, such informal or unofficial factors as (1) the society's historical heritage and geographic and resource endowments, its social and economic organization, its ideologies and value systems, and its political style; and (2) its party, interest, and leadership structure. Government, plus these two categories of related and mutually affective factors, thus constitutes the political system of a society.

The first step in the analysis of a given political system is to ascertain those aspects of a society's historical, geographical, social, economic, and ideological heritage and endowment—listed under category (1) above—which are significantly related to its political decision-making system. This will provide both a picture of the working environment of a system's politics and an inventory of the basic problems, resources, attitudes, groups, political alignments, and styles of action which relate to its political decision making. For this reason, we refer to such factors in the chapters which fellow as "the foundations of politics."

In practice it is not easy to agree, for a given society, on just which of its many characteristics are of present and primary political importance—that is, "foundational"—and which are of only historical or secondary importance. They are not necessarily the same from country to country, nor are they constant for different stages in the history of a single society. Their satisfactory identification and evaluation in any given case is itself a matter which calls for considerable study and sophistication and about which judgments will differ. In general, however, the more unfamiliar, non-Western, and underdeveloped the political system under consideration, the greater the need for explicit and detailed treatment of these foundational aspects of politics. American students simply do not bring to the study of Middle Eastern politics a fund of relevant information or a semi-intuitive "feel" for the situation in any way comparable to that which they bring to the study of their own or some Western European political system. Finally, it should be emphasized that these "foundations of politics," although they are here distinguished from one another, categorized, and treated separately, in fact constitute a unified, national, interrelated, and interactive complex. Their separation here for expository purposes should not lead one to forget this fact.

The interaction between these foundational aspects of a political system and the governmental organs of that system constitute "the dynamics of politics." Social, economic, political, and ideological claims and supports rising from these foundational aspects of a system are constantly being presented to officials and organs of government with the demand that they be converted into public policy. Political parties, interest or pressure groups, and political leaders play the role of conveyor belts between the makers of such claims and the organs of government which make official decisions and establish public policy. They thus serve as active or dynamic agents within a political system, sifting and choosing among the claims which demand action, formulating these in viable terms, gathering support, and presenting the results in the form of demands for political action. These dynamic factors of politics—political parties, interest or pressure groups, and political leaders—thus bridge the intrasystem gap between the political foundations and the formal decision-making organs of government.

The third major component of political systems is government, which is the formal and legitimacy-conferring machinery for the identification and posing of problems and the making and administering of decisions in the realm of public affairs. More specifically, it is the legislative, executive, judicial, and administrative or bureaucratic machinery of state, and the constitutional and legal framework within which these operate. Although distinctive functions and organs of these sorts are usually identifiable in most nonprimitive societies, it should not be assumed that they will be neatly and individually institutionalized along the lines indicated by these traditional categories or that they actually perform the functions indicated. Legislative and executive functions, for example, are often combined, and modern legislatures in practice seldom legislate in the complete, classical sense of that term. It should also be noted that for totalitarian systems such as the U.S.S.R. or the Chinese People's Republic it is largely meaningless to attempt to distinguish between the governmental roles and powers of the Communist Party and the formal apparatus of state.

In studying any system, we are interested in both the input and the output aspects of its mechanism. Consequently, for a given political system we are interested not only in the previously described "input" process by which it poses, makes, and administers its decisions but also in the nature, quality, and effectiveness of the decisions taken—that is, in the efficiency and performance characteristics of political systems as well as in their mechanics. The "output," or efficiency, of a political system can be gaged by its capacity to survive and by its ability to make decisions that are widely accepted. Assessment of the former is relatively simple. The latter, in a democratic system, can usually be determined by the response which its decisions elicit from social groups, interest groups, and other associations. In a totalitarian system, the test is similar, though the nature of the groups concerned and the manner of ascertaining their responses are different.

An efficient political system maintains a balance between stability and change. Change is an inevitable consequence of the competing political claims that arise among groups as a result of shifting technical, social, and economic conditions and of the demands that such groups press as they struggle to gain positions of influence and power. Efficiency, therefore, is a function of governmental response to such groups and demands. To be efficient, however, such a response must take place within a context of stable and generally accepted political institutions. Otherwise, emerging groups will attempt to gain power by revolutionary means, which have disruptive effects upon the entire system. From this point of view, there is no guarantee that a democratic political system is more efficient than a totalitarian one.

In the chapters that follow, this question of governmental efficiency will be discussed primarily in terms of two aspects of governmental performance. The author is concerned first with matters of relatively short-term performance. How do Middle Eastern governments define their appropriate spheres of political concern and activity? How do they allocate attention, funds, and resources among these spheres of concern? Beyond such relatively specific and short-term issues, however, we are also concerned with certain long-term performance characteristics of political systems. How efficiently have Middle Eastern countries coped with the larger problems of political development and modernization? What forms of political organization and action—democratic, authoritarian, or variants of these—have they found most appropriate to their needs? In whose behalf is the system operating? These are the underlying and enduring problems of all political systems in our time. Their import and urgency will vary within a particular system as well as from system to system, but some combination of these problems is critical for all societies. Together, they provide major themes for all the volumes of this series.

So much, then, for the manner in which we visualize our tasks. We have defined a political system as a mechanism for the identification and posing of problems and the making and administering of decisions in the realm of public affairs. We have established certain broad categories of analysis for such systems: political foundations, political dynamics, the formal decision-making organs of government on the input side of the process, and governmental efficiency and performance, both short-run and long-run, on the output side. In the chapters that follow, an attempt will be made to apply these categories in such a way as to illuminate the functioning and performance of the political systems of the Middle East.

ROBERT E. WARD
ROY C. MACRIDIS

PREFACE

This book seeks to provide a concise introduction to a region that has baffled both students and practitioners of its politics with its complex heritage and endemic turbulence. It avoids the self-conscious jargon recently fashionable among social scientists and, I hope, will present no difficulty for the beginner. Still, its manner of treatment and convenient factual synopses should make it of interest also to those more knowledgeable about the Middle East.

In contrast to other endeavors to present the politics of the region, the materials here are not organized on a country-by-country basis. Rather a systematic outline has been adopted, corresponding to other volumes in this series, that proceeds from a discussion of the geographic, socioeconomic, and historic foundations of Middle Eastern politics to an analysis of present political dynamics. Within this framework each chapter takes up both broad regional similarities and the variations that occur in individual political systems. Modernization—the painful adaptation of a traditional and religiously sanctioned way of life to the exigencies of a technological and organizational age—provides a central theme. The bitter political conflicts of the region, whether international or domestic, are presented in a mode characterized less by Olympian detachment than by an attempt at sympathetic understanding of the intensely human concerns involved on all sides.

A number of tables supplement the text and convey to the reader a goodly amount of factual information not readily available in such compact form: a list of major changes of political regime in each of the countries from the time it attained its current territorial identity to the present, a synopsis of the linguistic and religious composition of each state, figures on current petroleum production and revenues, and detailed data on party alignments and strengths in the elections and parliaments of the area's only two democracies, Israel and Turkey. An appendix brings together more conventional statistical data on the population, economy, and level of education of the region's fifteen political units, as well as comparative date for India, Japan, Russia, and the United States. A selected bibliography invites the reader to further study.

The presentation draws heavily on my chapter on "Southwest Asia" in the volume entitled *Modern Political Systems: Asia*, edited by Robert E. Ward and Roy C. Macridis and published by Prentice-Hall in 1963. But its scope has been substantially expanded by the inclusion of Egypt and the addition of material recounting the often revolutionary transformations of the 1960s.

It remains to express my thanks to Professor Ward and to the editorial staff at Prentice-Hall, particularly Roger Emblen and Barbara Christenberry, for their patience with a laggard manuscript, and to Mr. Sabri Sayari and Miss Sharon Zukin for research assistance, particularly with respect to the updating of the tables. As the author, I naturally bear full responsibility for such shortcomings of fact and interpretation as remain.

DANKWART A. RUSTOW
July 1970

CONTENTS

Chapter *1*

Introduction

Few major world regions have had as prominent a place in the newspaper headlines of the last two decades as the Middle East. In 1945, the Soviets' refusal to withdraw their wartime occupation forces from the Iranian province of Azarbayjan led to the first postwar clash between the Eastern and Western blocs—and the first use of the Soviet veto in the United Nations Security Council. The termination of the British mandate in Palestine in 1948 precipitated a war between the newly proclaimed state of Israel and its Arab neighbors. A few years later, the tearful, raging, pajama-clad figure of Dr. Muhammad Musaddiq [1] became a familiar sight to the news-

[1] A note on the spelling of Middle Eastern names in this section may forestall possible confusion. Turkish names and words are given in the official orthography employed since the change from Arabic to Latin alphabet in 1928. Arabic and Persian, on the other hand, continue to be written in the Arabic script. Hence names and words from these languages are given according to the transliteration system commonly employed by librarians and scholars in the United States, although diacritical marks (dots below and lines above some of the letters) and most of the apostrophes of the official transliteration have been omitted. This results at times in spellings that differ somewhat from the haphazard practice of the daily press. The reader will have little difficulty, however, in identifying names such as Abd Allah, Abdülhamid, Azarbayjan, Kuwayt, Musaddiq, Qasim, Qur'an, shaykh, and Uman even though he may previously have encountered them in the guise of Abdullah, Abdul Hamid, Azerbaijan, Kuwait, Mossadegh, Kassim, Koran, sheik, Oman, or the like. Only for a very few names, mostly of countries and cities, has a concession been made to well-established Western usage: Aden, Beirut, Mosul, Nasser, Saud, Tehran, Yemen instead of the more accurate Adan, Bayrut, Mawsil, Nasir, Suud, Tahran, Yaman.

1

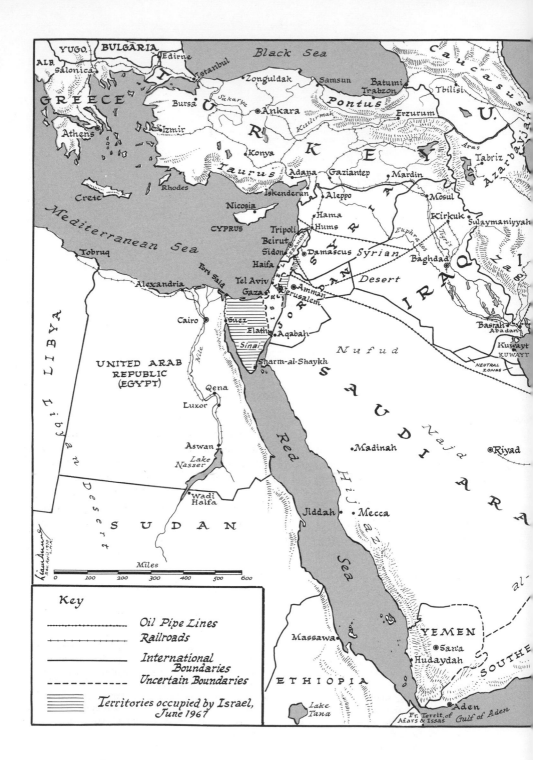

Key

‐‐‐‐‐‐‐‐‐	Oil Pipe Lines
┼┼┼┼┼┼	Railroads
——————	International Boundaries
‑ ‑ ‑ ‑ ‑ ‑	Uncertain Boundaries
▤▤▤	Territories occupied by Israel, June 1967

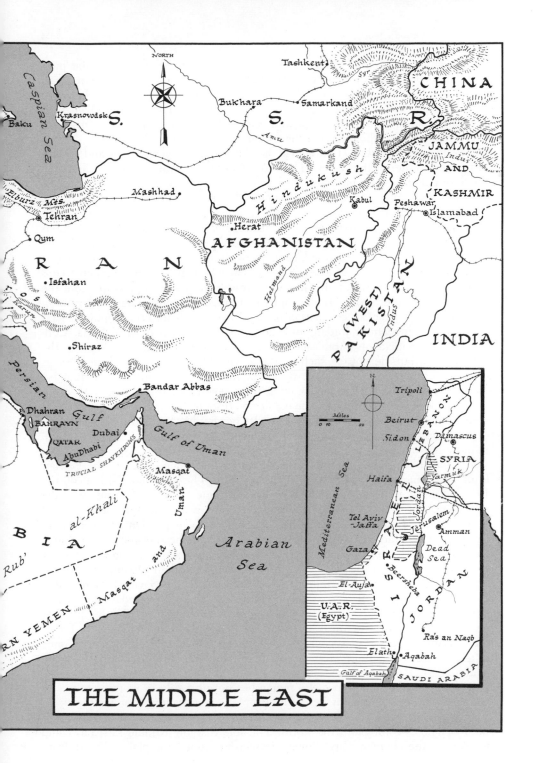

THE MIDDLE EAST

paper-reading public; his nationalization of Iranian oil led to one of the most protracted showdowns ever staged over the control of foreign investment in an "underdeveloped" country's natural resources. In 1958, a civil war in Lebanon led to the dispatch of United States Marines. Another civil war, in Yemen in the early sixties, embroiled Egypt and Saudi Arabia, and military coups have been endemic throughout most of the region.

The most serious conflict, of course, has been that between Arabs and Israelis at the very center of the region. The Zionist ideal to establish a Jewish national home in Palestine after millennia of dispersion and persecution clashed with the aspirations of Arab nationalists to whom the very existence of Israel became a symbol of humiliation and defeat. Three times, in 1948, 1956, and 1967, the smoldering conflict erupted into open warfare, and each time the United Nations and individual outside powers were profoundly involved. The first Arab-Israeli War in 1948 resulted in the establishment of the State of Israel. The second, in 1956, brought Israeli forces to the Suez Canal where British and French troops soon joined the attack; but all three withdrew in response to pressure from the United States, the Soviet Union, and the United Nations. The third war, in June 1967, left Israel in occupation of the Sinai Peninsula, the populous west bank of the kingdom of Jordan, and the strategic Golan heights in Syria. Continual frontier incidents, Arab sabotage, and Israeli retaliation raids kept up the tension, and outside powers such as the Soviet Union and the United States continued to be closely involved. By 1970, there was an almost daily duel between Israeli and Egyptian jets, some of them flown by Russian pilots.

The Arab-Israeli conflict and many lesser disputes testify to the paramount strategic importance of the Middle East. Its geographic location makes it a link or a barrier between two oceans and among three continents. Commerce traditionally has moved in an east-west direction. In the Middle Ages, Far Eastern spices and silks reached Europe via trade routes that came by sea to the Persian Gulf and hence overland to the Mediterranean. The so-called life-line of the British Empire followed the same approximate route—from India and Australia via Aden, Suez, and Gibraltar to England. And since the First and Second World Wars, European industry has become vitally dependent on petroleum shipped by pipeline or tanker from the area around the head of the Persian Gulf. In a north-south direction, the Middle East has been a major potential barrier to Russian expansion toward the Mediterranean, the Indian Ocean, and Africa. Southwest Asia is, notably, the only area adjacent to the Soviet Union where Communist power still is contained within its pre-1945 boundaries. Massive Soviet shipments of arms after 1955 and again after the war of 1967 for the first time created a Soviet political and military presence in the region. "As far as sheer value of territory is concerned," General Dwight D. Eisenhower once stated, "there is no more strategically important area in the world than the Middle East."

But the political importance of a region lies not primarily in its trade routes or strategic positions. Rather it lies in its people—their traditions and aspirations, their hopes and fears, and their patterns of interaction among themselves and with their neighbors throughout the world. The role that the Middle East has come to play on the contemporary diplomatic scene cannot be explained apart from the region's domestic political forces. And the internal political situation in the Middle East, like that in most of the so-called developing areas—reflects the intense, at time chaotic, interplay of forces of tradition and modernity.

The Middle East offers a particularly instructive laboratory for a comparative study of the process of political modernization. It includes traditional patriarchal societies such as Afghanistan and Yemen, which have as yet been barely touched by the industrial revolution of production and transport. It includes Saudi Arabia, where a modern petroleum industry is starkly juxtaposed with a tribal society of Bedouin camel herders. It includes societies such as Iraq and Iran which are in intense political and social turmoil. It includes Turkey which, aside from Japan, has pursued a more drastic policy of rapid cultural change than any other country of Asia. It includes Egypt, where recurrent efforts at modernization since the early nineteenth century were gravely hampered by imperialist interference and then by overpopulation. And it includes Israel, where an immigrant population has laid the foundation for a modern pluralistic society in a hostile physical and international environment.

Two basic aspects of contemporary Middle Eastern politics particularly merit the close attention of the student. The first aspect is the emergence of new states. The region includes three countries which have a well-defined historical identity —Turkey, Iran, Afghanistan. But throughout the rest of the Middle East, the basic political units were first conceived and created in the present century, in the aftermath of the First and Second World Wars. The second aspect is the psychological ambivalence of Middle Easterners toward modern European and Western civilization. Of all the "non-Western" regions of the world, the Middle East has been the one culturally and geographically closest to Europe. The conquests of Alexander, the rise of Christianity, the Crusades, and the rise and fall of the Ottoman Empire testify to the closeness of the connection. Yet Middle Eastern experience with European imperialism was of a particularly unpleasant sort, largely because European expansion into the area came late, at a time when Europeans were beset by apologetic second thoughts about imperialism as the "white man's burden" and when much of the Middle Eastern elite had already been converted to Western ideals of nationality and constitutionalism. The recent emergence of basic political units accounts for the prevalent insecurity not only of boundaries but also of political loyalties. And the late and unhappy experience with Western imperialism accounts for the intense mixture of admiration and hate of the West which is so widespread among urban Middle Easterners. Both facts, in turn, have decisively contributed to the explosive instability of the recent Middle Eastern political scene.

The Middle East is located at the intersection of the three continents of the Old World with branches of two major oceans, and throughout history it has been a passageway for cultural influences and an arena for conflicting political interests. It is a logical consequence of this focal location that there should be no general agreement as to the precise boundaries of the region. The leading scholarly periodical *The Middle East Journal* holds that the Middle East encompasses all countries from Morocco to Sinkiang and India and from Transcaucasia to Ethiopia and the Sudan. Others have applied the term Middle East (or Near East, as it also is often called) to a much more limited area. This work conforms to prevailing usage in that it includes those countries that are likely to be part of anyone's Middle East: Egypt, the Arab countries of Asia, Israel, Turkey, Iran, and Afghanistan.[2]

[2] For a lively and informative discussion of the multitude of terms and definitions that have been employed see Roderic H. Davison, "Where Is the Middle East?" *Foreign Affairs* (July 1960), reprinted in R. H. Nolte, ed., *The Modern Middle East* (New York: Atherton Press, Inc., 1963), pp. 13–29.

Chapter 2

The Foundations of Politics
HISTORY

The Traditional Middle East and Its Decline

Two features, above all, are characteristic of the historical legacy of Middle Eastern politics—the tradition of empire and autocracy, and the tradition of local particularism. The Middle East was the site of the most highly developed ancient civilizations—those of the old Egyptians in the Nile Valley and Delta; of the Sumerians, Babylonians, and Assyrians in Mesopotamia, the "Land Between the Rivers" (Euphrates and Tigris); of the Hittites in the highlands of Anatolia; and of the ancient Persians on the Iranian plateau. Egyptians, Mesopotamians, and Iranians took turns erecting vast empires throughout the region. Alexander of Macedonia, Hulagu the Mongol, Timur (or Tamerlane) the Turk, and other conquerors invaded the Middle East from adjacent regions. All of them combined military talent with a supreme disregard for human lives. Many of them displayed a taste for monumental architecture and public works—pyramids, roads, dams and canals, and palaces. Yet the more spectacular the rise of an empire, the more rapid, as a rule, was its decline.

In contrast to the history of China, no geographically fixed concept of the Middle East emerged. The constituent units, such as Egypt, Syria, Mesopotamia, Persia, and Anatolia reasserted their identity, separated as they were in many instances by vast stretches of desert. Even under the rule of a single monarch, the various cities, towns, and villages retained much *de facto* autonomy. The nomadic tribes of the desert fringes through most of history remained each a law unto itself and a perennial threat to its sedentary neighbors. The difficulties of transport and of social organization generally restricted the effective rule of emperors, kings, and sultans to their palaces and capital cities or to their army camps. Only in the fertile river valleys—above all in Egypt and to a lesser extent in Mesopotamia—did the common needs of irrigation lay the basis for a tradition of bureaucratic organization.

The conquest that was to leave the deepest and most lasting impact on the Middle East was one that proceeded from the center of the region, Arabia. Yet the Arab conquest was less notable for its political than for its cultural and religious consequences. The austere monotheism preached by Muhammad (570–632 A.D.) in the trading towns of Mecca and Madinah briefly caused the surrounding Bedouin tribes to forget their mutual raids and feuds. In the name of Islam they conquered, within a century after the Prophet's death, a vast area from Spain to northwest India. While the political empire of Muhammad's successors, the Caliphs, crumbled, most of its inhabitants retained their Muslim religion—and, on that basis, a distinct if variegated Middle Eastern civilization.

Islam served to establish a measure of unity throughout the region—and on a more effective and lasting basis than the previous imperial conquests. In the medieval heyday of Islamic civilization, Muslims from Seville, Cairo, Baghdad, and Bukhara engaged in commercial and intellectual exchange, their allegiance to a common faith transcending any purely political loyalties. Yet Islam allowed not only for political divisiveness but also for cultural diversity. Islam does not prescribe a rigid orthodoxy within an elaborate theological doctrine. The profession of monotheism and of the prophecy of Muhammad, and the intention to carry out the major ritual observances (daily prayers, alms, fast, and pilgrimage) are the only essential requisites for membership in the Muslim community. The Muslim equivalent of a clergy, the *alims* (or, with the Arabic plural, *ulama*), are not a priesthood who form a strict autonomous hierarchy or whose ministrations are considered essential to salvation. Rather, they are "learned men," men who have acquired sufficient knowledge of the basic Islamic lore of law, ethics, and theology. What formal offices the ulama may hold they receive by appointment from the local community of believers (e.g., as imams, or prayer leaders) or from central political authority (e.g., as qadis or judges).

A great variety of sects and schools of legal interpretation thus could grow up without disrupting the basic unity of Islam. In fact, sectarian organization rapidly became the normal vehicle for the expression of political or social discontent. A particular form of Islamic religious organization which spread in the Middle Ages is that of the religious brotherhoods or dervish orders. Each of these consists of the brothers who have taken a set of ascetic vows or practice a mystical ritual, and of lay members. While many of these orders are limited to a particular country, others are widespread throughout the Muslim sphere. It has been estimated that today perhaps one Muslim out of 30 or 40 is a member of one of these orders, and it has been suggested that it was principally the rise of these orders (rather than any political continuity) which enable Islam to survive the twofold onslaught of the Turkish and Mongol invasions (tenth to fourteenth centuries).

Political strength was restored to the Islamic Middle East most notably as a result of the Ottoman conquests. The Ottomans started out in the thirteenth century as a Turkish warrior tribe on the Anatolian border of the Byzantine Empire. Their conquests spread spectacularly—first primarily in the Balkan and

Danubian areas of southeast Europe and then in the Arab Middle East. Süleyman the Magnificent (reigned 1520–66) ruled an empire from Hungary to Yemen and from the Caspian Sea to Algiers, without question the largest and most durable political structure to emerge west of the Himalayas after the fall of Rome.

Part of the secret of the rapid Arab conquest of the seventh and eighth centuries and of the later Ottoman conquests was the tolerant attitude of Islam toward other revealed religions. Christians and Jews, as "People of the Book," enjoy a special status as subjects of an Islamic ruler. So long as they recognize his rule and pay a poll tax, they are to be left free in the exercise of their religion—and (as we shall see in more detail in a latter section) the traditional Islamic conception draws no distinction between religion on the one hand, and law, social custom, and ethics, on the other. While most administrative and military positions are reserved to Muslims, there is no stigma on conversion, and, in fact, most of the highest positions in the Ottoman Empire were long held by Christian converts or their immediate descendants. While Christians and Jews mingled freely with Muslims in the Baghdad of the Caliphs, the Ottomans enforced a measure of social segregation; Christians and Jews had a virtual monopoly on trade, finance, and the arts and crafts, whereas Muslims monopolized the government and army at one end of the social scale and held the largest share of agriculture at the other. The Ottoman system of social segregation and legal autonomy of non-Muslims—known as the *millet* (or denominational) system—thus provided a form of legal decentralization which was added to the *de facto* decentralization imposed by imperfections of communication.

Even when the Ottoman Empire stood at its zenith, however, the long-range balance of power was beginning to tip toward Europe. The explorations of the fifteenth and sixteenth centuries not only opened the treasures of the New World to the Europeans, they also installed European power in India and later in Africa, thus effectively setting bounds to the further political expansion of Islam. Christendom, long the Western neighbor, had encircled the House of Islam from the South and the East. Meanwhile, the commercial and industrial revolutions and the rise of absolute monarchies and later of nation-states provided Europe with a level of technology and of political and social cohesion for which the Ottomans proved to be no match. Throughout the eighteenth century, the Ottomans retreated along the Danube and the northern Black Sea shore before Austrian and Russian armies. Napoleon's invasion of Egypt (1798–1801) was a piercing thrust whose long-range cultural and political repercussions far exceeded its immediate military effects. The fact that Nelson's British squadrons rather than Ottoman regiments clinched Napoleon's defeat was symbolic of the future. Even more portentous were the Westernizing reforms of the Ottoman governor of Egypt, Muhammad Ali (1805–49), which closely copied the military and industrial organization introduced under the French occupation and which enabled Egypt to make itself virtually independent of the Ottoman Empire. First as an ally and later as a declared antagonist of the Sultan, Muhammad Ali conquered large parts of the Ottoman Arab territories. Once again, it was the intervention of the European powers which saved the Ottoman Empire and limited Muhammad Ali to Egypt. The last and most powerful of the great Muslim empires was clearly in decline.

The Emergence of the Modern Middle East

The nineteenth century brought a phase of intensive and often violent interplay between forces of tradition and modernization (or, as it may properly be called in the Middle East, Westernization). Cumulative military defeat provided the initial stimulus for reform, but the movement soon went far beyond mere army reorganization. French military instructors were called to the Ottoman Empire in the late eighteenth century, and Prussian instructors (including the famed Helmuth von Moltke) followed in the nineteenth. But, as Egyptain experience had shown, the reformed army depended on industrial production for its supplies, and industrialization required increased and centralized taxation and a reform of the entire legal and administrative systems. The new army and the expanded civil service alike needed trained manpower, and a vast new network of Ottoman higher and secondary schools was created on the European model by the mid-nineteenth century to supply this need. In the Arab countries, in particular, the spread of Western-style education was furthered by American, French, and British missionary and philanthropic institutions; significantly, it was a Presbyterian mission school, the predecessor of today's American University of Beirut, which set up the first permanent Arab printing press in 1834. The new educational system in turn produced an elite committed to Westernization not only as a buttress to tradition and to the Sultan's power but as an end in itself—regardless of the Sultan and, increasingly, against the Sultan.

The modernizing elite's dissatisfaction with the Sultan and his autocratic rule was accentuated by the failure of the nineteenth-century reforms to yield any appreciable increase in military-political power. Defeat had piled on defeat, humiliation upon humiliation, and expense upon expense. With Europe's tacit or open support, the Ottomans' Balkan subjects had one by one attained independence. It was clearly only the rivalry of the European powers, particularly Britain and Russia, which kept any one of them from delivering the last crushing blow. By 1881, the collection of Ottoman customs revenues was turned over to the empire's European creditors. Similar developments had occured in Iran, where less effective but proportionately costlier measures of Westernization had depleted the treasury, while lucrative concessions for construction of public works or for trade monopolies had been bartered to European financiers. Increasingly, the educated elite became convinced that a representative constitution was needed to check the spendthrift and arbitrary power of sultan or shah. In the Ottoman Empire, the first organized political movements had their origins in this antiautocratic opposition of the mid-nineteenth century, and, significantly, the first nucleus was provided by students of the Army Medical School, the most highly Westernized unit among the reformed military services.

In Iran, on the other hand, the opposition was largely led by the Shii ulama, who organized a successful boycott of a British tobacco concession in the 1890s. The rapid growth of an indigenous press gave further impetus to the demands for political reform. Repression at home temporarily transferred the center of organization abroad, to the Ottoman exiles clustering around Cairo, Paris, and Geneva,

and to the Iranian ones around Calcutta. The adoption of the Ottoman Constitution of 1876 (reproclaimed after three decades of deliberate disregard under
Sultan Adbülhamid as a result of the so-called Young Turk Revolution of 1908)
and the Iranian Constitution of 1906 were the immediate results of this snow-
balling opposition.

But once again, internal reform was accompanied by a short-term decline,
rather than by a dramatic increase, in international power. In 1907, Britain and
Russia divided Iran into agreed spheres of political and economic influence, and
in the First World War, Russian, German, British, and Ottoman troops criss-
crossed Iran without anyone's troubling to declare war on her. The Ottoman
Empire in the Libyan and Balkan Wars (1911–13) lost its remaining European
and African possessions. The reckless entry of the Young Turk regime into the
First World War on the German side served to precipitate the final defeat of the
Ottoman Empire.

In Egypt, internal reform and external intervention became even more closely
interwoven. The cotton boom of the years of the American Civil War led to a
headlong rush of speculation and concession-hunting, and when the inevitable
bust followed, it was the Egyptian treasury rather than the European speculators
that was left holding the bag. In 1875 the Khedive (a title assumed by Muhammad Ali's successors) was forced to sell his shares in the newly opened (1868)
Suez Canal to Britain, and in 1878 to turn the collection of revenues over to a
European-controlled administration of the public debt. The attempt by rebellious
officers under Colonel Urabi in 1881 to impose parliamentary controls on the
spendthrift ruler suggested to Europeans the specter of default on Egypt's debt.
The net result was British military occupation of Egypt (1882), announced as
"temporary" but in fact maintained, in one form or another, for three-quarters
of a century.

Constitutionalism had been no more effective than autocratic reform in stav-
ing off disaster. But a far more potent force introduced into the Middle East
in the nineteenth century was nationalism, a force both for disruption and for
reconstruction. In Iran, the survival of Persian as a distinctive language with a
rich literary tradition and the emergence in the sixteenth century of Shii
(heterodox) Islam as a distinctive religious tradition made possible a continuous
and imperceptible transition from traditional patriotism to modern nationalism.
For the peoples of the Ottoman Empire—both Turks and Arabs—the change
was more abrupt and painful.

The empire was based on loyalty to the Ottoman dynasty—the descendants
of Osman—and to the social and cultural structure of Islam, with its assigned
niches for the subject "People of the Book." The needs of frontier warfare and
of commerce within an ethnic division of labor had led in many areas to a
checkerboard pattern of settlement, with Greek living next to Bulgarian and
Albanian, or Turk next to Arab, Armenian, and Kurd. Clearly, nationalism—the
demand that each of these nationalities form a distinct political state—cut at
the very ideological and social foundations of the empire. The Balkan Christians
were the first to take over the nationalist ideology of Christain Europe, and their
quest for independence was actively supported by European power. Among the
Muslims of the empire, nationalism was long sternly and instinctively resisted.
The Westernized Ottoman elite of the nineteenth century attempted to instill

in the empire's subjects an Ottoman patriotism that would be transreligious as well as transnational. It is significant that the nineteenth-century political exiles whom the Europeans called "Young Turks" referred to themselves as "New Ottomans" and that some Arab and Armenian delegates took part in their congresses. Subtly and gradually, however, Ottomanism was in practice converted into Turkish nationalism; thus the newly founded civil service and military training schools showed in their admissions policies a distinct bias not only for the Muslims generally but specifically for the Turkish element, and the insistence on Turkish as the language of secondary education did much to antagonize the Muslim Albanians who had thus far been the Ottomans' most loyal Balkan subjects. Yet it was not until the calamity of the Balkan wars that the terms "Turk" and "Turkish" gained intellectual respectability among the Ottoman elite, and not until the early 1920s that the conversion from an Ottoman to a Turkish political consciousness was completed.

The idea of Arab nationalism came just as late; with the rapid decline of Ottoman political fortunes it spread faster, although the support for Arab nation-statehood was not nearly as widespread in the Syrian and Iraqi provinces of the defeated Ottoman Empire as present-day nationalist spokesmen would have us believe. Even less was there any vocal or organized support for Pan-Arabism, the ideal of political unity for all Arab-speaking peoples of northern Africa and Southwest Asia. For example, an Egyptain nationalist leader, when approached at the Paris Peace Conference of 1918–20 on behalf of the Arabs of the defunct Ottoman Empire, insisted that "our problem is an Egyptian problem and not an Arab problem.

For the Turkish rump of the Ottoman Empire, defeat in the First World War was followed by victory in the Turkish War of Independence, fought against Allied partition plans generally and more specifically against Greek plans to resurrect a latter-day Byzantine Empire. Victory, in turn, laid the psychological and political foundations for rapid Westernization in Atatürk's newly created Turkish Republic. For the Arabs to the south, hopes for unity and independence were quickly shattered. Vague and alluring wartime promises of Allied support for Arab aspirations were converted into the grim reality of partition and foreign rule. In Egypt, the British military occupation in 1914 was converted into a protectorate, coupled with the promise of postwar independence. But when "independence" came, in 1922, it was hedged about with so many conditions reserving British control of foreign and military affairs that the declaration of it had to be issued unilaterally in London over Egyptian protests. In the Fertile Crescent (i.e., Palestine including the later states of Israel and Jordan, Syria-Lebanon, and Iraq), the violent measures required to impose these new regimes clearly belied the lofty educational theory of the mandate. The opening of Palestine to Jewish immigration under Britain's wartime policy of support for Zionism (the famous Balfour Declaration of 1917) further wounded Arab pride, for here mandate administration meant not only foreign colonial rule but also foreign colonization.

Only on the Arabian peninsula did independent Arab states emerge from the aftermath of the World War. In the desert interior, the belligerent Wahhabi-sect of Islam under King Ibn Saud subdued the neighboring tribes and, in 1926, conquered the Hijaz and thus unified most of the peninsula. Remote Yemen gained its independence without any formal diplomatic ceremony, by virtue mainly of its inaccessibility to great-power conflict.

The people of Egypt and the Fertile Crescent, on the other hand, soon learned that, just as the mandates had been installed by force, only force, exerted by the Arabs themselves or by outsiders, could be counted on to bring about any decisive modification in the system of foreign rule. The history of the French mandate in Syria, of the British mandate in Palestine, and of Iraq both before and after termination of the mandate was punctuated by uprisings such as the Druze revolt in Southern Syria, the Rashid Ali coup in Iraq in 1941, and the recurrent waves of terrorism in the 1940s of Arab and Jewish groups in Palestine.

In Egypt, abortive negotiations to regularize the pseudoindependence of 1922 dragged on until 1936, when the threat of Italian expansion in the Mediterranean and Ethiopia drew the British and the nationalist Wafd party closer together. Toward the beginning of the Second World War, the government of the youthful King Faruq leaned toward the Axis powers, until British tanks surrounding the royal palace forced the return of the Wafd.

During the Second World War and in the years immediately following, the combination of internal and external strains also undermined the structure of British and French domination of the Fertile Crescent. As a result of Ottoman defeat in the First World War, the Arabs of Southwest Asia had shaken off Turkish rule; as a result of the weakening of Western Europe in the Second World War, they attained full independence.

Iran did not assert her independence in a dramatic military effort like Turkey and escaped the foreign rule to which most of the Arab states were subjected. Nevertheless, a treaty that would have made Iran a virtual British protectorate was signed in 1919, although never ratified by the Iranian Parliament. In both world wars, moreover, foreign troops operated freely on Iranian territory, and after each war, a Soviet-inspired secessionist regime was briefly installed in the north. The contest in 1951–53 over nationalization of Iran's British-owned petroleum resources, moreover, revealed and released many of the xenophobic nationalist passions familiar in colonial settings.

In the more remote countries of the Middle East—such as Afghanistan and the smaller states of the Arabian peninsula—the forces of modernization have intruded only since the Second World War or even more recently. In Kuwayt and the other Persian Gulf states, the discovery and production of petroleum has been the decisive factor. Elsewhere it was the extension of American and Russian foreign aid as a result of the cold war of the 1950s that furnished the chief impetus (Yemen, Afghanistan).

Before examining the more detailed impact of all these forces on the politics of each major country of the region, it is time to survey the social and economic background of the region (chap. 3) and the ideologies that animate its rulers and its politically active citizens (chap. 4).

Chapter *3*

The Foundations of Politics
ECOLOGICAL AND
SOCIAL STRUCTURE

Geographic Foundations

The Middle East, as defined in this book, has roughly the shape of an equilateral triangle pointed southward, with the air distance from Istanbul in the northwest to Kabul in the northeast, and from each of these to Aden in the south being around 2,500 miles. But the regularity of the triangle's shape is interrupted by several major bodies of water: the Persian Gulf in the east, up to 200 miles wide and about 600 miles long and connecting with the Indian Ocean through the Gulf of Uman; the Red Sea in the south, even narrower and twice as long, dividing the Asian parts of the Middle East from Egypt; the eastern part of the Mediterranean in the west; and the Black and Caspian seas bordering on the region in the north. There are high mountains in the northern third of the region forming two parallel chains (known as the Pontus and Taurus in Turkey and the Elburz and Zagros in Iran) intertwined in the Armenian Knot (eastern Turkey) and the Hindukush (eastern Afghanistan), which are part of the giant tertiary fold stretching from the Alps to the Himalayas. Two older mountain massifs are located at the two tips of the Arabian peninsula (Yemen and Uman), and a smaller series of mountain ranges (the Lebanon and Anti-Lebanon) line the eastern Mediterranean coast. There is a narrow but deep trough, beginning as the Jordan Valley and continuing as the Dead Sea (a salty inland lake whose surface is 1,300 feet below sea level), which is part of one of the major geological faults on the globe, connecting southward with the Red Sea and the East African lakes (Albert and Tanganyika).

The location of seas and mountains determines the region's climate. In most

14

places where moist winds come from the sea, their passage is blocked by major mountains. Thus there is abundant rainfall along the coast of Uman (in the monsoon season), along the Caspian slope of the Elburz and the Black Sea slope of the Pontus mountains; there is adequate rainfall around the Mediterranean coast, whereas no clouds cross the flat coastlines of the Red Sea and the Persian Gulf. The only major rivers of the region are the Nile, the world's longest river, carrying the waters of the Ethiopian and Ugandan highlands and of the swamps of the southern Sudan across the Egyptian desert; the Euphrates and the Tigris, flowing from the Armenian mountains to the Persian Gulf, with a number of lesser streams in Turkey and in southwestern Iran. Most of the rest of the region, notably the Iranian plateau and the Arabian peninsula, and, of course, Egypt, is steppe or desert lacking rainfall and rivers.

Geography and climate thus divide the Middle East into four distinct parts. (1) The northern mountain belt of Turkey, Iran, and Afghanistan with its fertile coastal plains and generally arid interior. (2) The so-called Fertile Crescent, an arc of arable land stretching from Palestine in the southwest along the Levant coast (Lebanon and western Syria) to northern Syria and Iraq. Inside this arc and south of it is the Syrian desert, including southern Syria, southwestern Iraq, and most of Jordan. Further west, the Euphrates and Tigris provide an immense and largely unused irrigation potential for what the ancient Greeks called the "Land Between the Rivers" (Mesopotamia) and the Arabs call "the Island" (al-Jazirah), i.e., northern Syria and most of Iraq. (3) The Arabian peninsula, most of it alternating between steppe and desert. The Nufud desert in the north adjoins the Syrian desert. The stony waste that occupies the eastern third of the peninsula is known appropriately as "the Empty Quarter" (al-Rub' al-Khali). Elsewhere, the desert is interrupted by oases and small fertile stretches. In the mountains of Yemen, at the peninsula's southern tip, there is enough rainfall for terrace agriculture. (4) Egypt, consisting of two narrow strips of fertile land flanking the banks of the Nile, flaring out into the Delta with its crisscross of streams and canals, but surrounded right and left by hundreds of miles of sandy or stony desert.

Mineral deposits in the Middle East are distributed as unevenly as is water and topsoil. In Turkey, there are small deposits of coal and iron ore, and more substantial ones of chromium and manganese. Potash is produced in Israel at the southern end of the Dead Sea. By far the most important mineral of the region is its petroleum (Table 3-1), with presently known deposits concentrated at the northern end of the Persian Gulf (the al-Hasa costal region of Saudi Arabia, the shaykhdom of Kuwayt, the Basrah region of Iraq, and the Abadan region of southwestern Iran). A number of smaller pools surround this central petroleum region within a 500-mile radius: Mosul and Kirkuk in northern Iraq, Khanikin at the Iraqi-Iranian border, Qum in north-central Iran, the island of Bahrayn, Qatar, Abu Dhabi, Dubai, and the Buraymi oasis along the Saudi Uman border. Together, these Southwest Asian petroleum deposits account for about two-thirds of the proven reserves on the globe. Intensive prospecting in various parts of the world continues to change this picture. Recent oil discoveries in Algeria, Libya, and Alaska, for example, have reduced the share of the Middle East in the known world total. On the other hand, petroleum deposits in the Persian Gulf region have been so abundant that only the most immediately promising areas have been exploited or even systematically prospected. Exploratory drilling continues in a number of new Middle Eastern locations, such as southeastern Turkey, Egypt, Yemen, and the submarine shelf of the Persian Gulf —and any new gusher brought in may change the comparative estimates overnight.

Economic Foundations

Primary production predominates in the economy of the Middle East. A vast majority of the population—probably around four-fifths of it—derives its livelihood from agriculture and husbandry, and the most lucrative source of income for the region is its petroleum deposits. There is cereal farming, mainly of wheat, in Turkey, Syria, and Iran. Dates are grown in Iraq (which accounts for about 80 per cent of world production) and form the main staple of the desert and steppe population of the Arabian peninsula. Sheep and goats are a major source of meat and milk in the entire region; these join with cattle and water buffalo (for meat and milk and as draft animals) in the north. In the desert and steppe areas, the camel is the chief traditional resource—for transport, for milk, and for meat.

More differentiated soil products are grown chiefly in the irrigated Nile Valley and along the rain-fed coasts of the Mediterranean. Northern Turkey supplies most of the hazelnuts available on the world market. The Izmir region of western Turkey produces tobacco, figs, and raisins. Lebanon and Israel have become major citrus exporters and produce many other fruits and vegetables. Cotton is the mainstay of the Egyptian economy.

The Egyptian economy shows what human ingenuity and determination can do to change ecological factors. Since there is no rainfall, all agriculture is based on the waters of the Nile, which have been spread over a wider area by irrigation since Pharaonic times. A series of dams built in the nineteenth century made it possible to grow two or three crops per year over an even wider area. And the gigantic High Dam at Aswan, completed with Russian aid in the 1960s increased the agricultural capacity even further. Elsewhere there is unused irrigation potential in the Khuzistan region of southeastern Iran, and also in the region between the rivers of Iraq and Syria. In many areas, however, drainage is an even more urgent requirement in order to prevent the constantly increasing salinity of the soil.

The only abundant economic asset of the Middle East is its oil. Middle Eastern petroleum is plentiful, it is cheap, and it makes a major contribution to the public finance of the countries where it is found. The known reserves of the region, at current rates of pumping, may be expected to last for a hundred years, and there is little question that any significant increase in demand would lead to more extensive exploration. Middle Eastern petroleum prospecting, in other words, keeps a century ahead of current demand, whereas in places such as Texas and Louisiana that ratio is about a dozen years. As a result of these favorable economic factors, Middle Eastern oil is highly competitive on the world market. With full allowance made for importing machinery and managerial personnel from Europe and America and for transporting the oil across the

TABLE 3-1

PETROLEUM IN THE MIDDLE EAST AND NORTH AFRICA, 1967

COUNTRY	PRODUCTION OF CRUDE PETROLEUM (millions of barrels per year)	(percentage of world total)	PROVED RESERVES (billions of barrels)	(percentage of world total)	GOVERNMENT REVENUES FROM PETROLEUM (millions of $ per year)	OWNERSHIP OF PRODUCING COMPANIES BY NATIONALITY AND PERCENTAGE OF PRODUCTION U.S.	British	British-Dutch	French	Other
Saudi Arabia	948.1	7.6	77.0	19.3	843	100	—	—	—	—
Iran	947.7	7.4	43.0	10.3	746	40	40	14	6	1
Kuwayt	836.7	6.5	70.0	17.5	710	50	50	—	—	—
Iraq	448.0	3.4	29.0	7.3	362	24	24	24	24	5
Neutral Zone	151.5	1.2	12.0	3.0	—a	100	—	—	—	—
Abu Dhabi b	139.2	1.1	8.0	2.0	—	8	55	8	29	2
Qatar	118.2	.9	3.6	.9	227	24	24	24	24	5
Bahrayn	25.4	.2	.4	.1	—	—	—	—	—	—
Egypt	39.6	.3	1.8	.5	—	—	—	—	—	—
Uman	23.0	.2	2.0	.5	—	—	85	—	—	15
Syria	—	—	1.0	.2	—	—	—	—	—	—
Dubai b	—	—	1.0	.2	—	—	—	—	—	—
Turkey	19.5	.2	.8	.2	—	—	—	—	—	—
Israel	1.0	.008	.01	.0	—	—	—	—	—	—
Middle East	3697.8	29.0	249.5	62.0	2,888	57	28	7	6	2
Libya	636.5	4.9	20.0	5.0	625	—	—	—	—	—
Algeria	302.8	2.4	6.9	1.7	—	—	—	—	—	—
Tunisia	17.5	.1	.4	.1	—	—	—	—	—	—
Morocco	.7	.006	.01	.0	—	—	—	—	—	—
Middle East and North Africa	4655.4	37.4	276.8	69.3	—	—	—	—	—	—

Sources: *World Oil* and *Petroleum Press Service*.
a One half included in Kuwayt, one half in Saudi Arabia.
b Trucial shaykhdoms.

Atlantic, Middle Eastern oil is cheap enough to have brought into play various restrictive measures to reduce its share of the American market. Elsewhere, the Middle East supplies more than half of the European and more than four-fifths of the Japanese demand.

Petroleum is equally abundant in Algeria and in Libya, which, like the other North African countries, share in the historical and cultural heritage of the Arab Middle East and from where transport costs to Europe are even lower. Just before the 1967 Arab-Israeli war, petroleum also was beginning to be discovered in sizable quantities in Egypt along the Gulf of Suez.

The proceeds of this lucrative production are now in excess of $5 billion annually, and since the early 1950s such profits have been divided equally between American- or European-owned companies and the host governments. They now provide practically all the public revenues of Saudi Arabia, Kuwayt, and Bahrayn, and a major proportion of revenues in Iraq and Iran. In addition, transit dues from pipelines traversing Syria and canal dues from tankers passing Suez are a significant source of income for Syria and Egypt. Jordan and Lebanon also benefit from the Trans-Arabian Pipeline (TAP-Line) which connects the Saudi fields with the Mediterranean. The pipeline from Kirkuk, Iraq, to Haifa, Israel, has been out of operation since the Arab-Israeli War of 1948. With the closing of the canal after the 1967 war, the Arab oil countries have compensated Egypt with a special subsidy.

Important as petroleum is for the public finance of some of the countries, its contribution to the region's industrialization is somewhat limited. We commonly speak of an oil "industry," but it is clear that petroleum production is an extractive, primary production process. The oil fields themselves and the construction of pipelines serve to stimulate some branches of the construction industry and provide employment for local technical and maintenance personnel. Some of the petroleum produced around the Persian Gulf is refined in the region itself, the largest installations being at Ras Tanura, Saudi Arabia, on Bahrayn, at Abadan, at Kuwayt, and at Aden, thus giving rise to further industrial employment.

But with all this—and despite the conscious efforts of the oil companies to delegate a maximum of technical and managerial tasks to local employees—the oil industry necessarily remains something of a foreign body in the economics of the region, particularly in Saudi Arabia and the Gulf shaykhdoms. Petroleum exploration and production were stimulated solely by demand from other industrialized world regions. The capital and the machinery needed for exploration, drilling, and refining continue to come from the outside, as does the higher-level technical and managerial personnel. Of the profits, half go abroad to the operating companies. The other half is spent, in Iraq and Iran, on various economic development projects—irrigation, road building, and the like. The Kuwayti revenues finance one of the most complete welfare state systems on the globe. The Saudi revenues very largely go into lavish living for the royal family, its entourage, and tribal leaders who once paid tribute to the king but now are rewarded handsomely for loyal conduct. The private fortunes thus made directly or indirectly on oil are likely to be spent on products of European and American industry such as automobiles and refrigerators, unproductively invested in luxurious apartment buildings in Beirut, or put away in anonymous bank accounts in London, Zurich, or New York.

Petroleum revenues have had their most notable impact on Iran, where they have financed the Shah's "white revolution"—an ambitious program of agrarian reform designed to mobilize peasant support as a counterweight against the restless urban middle class.

The experience of the Middle East thus indicates that a lucrative extractive industry will not automatically transform a desert camel-and-date economy into a thriving modern industrial society. In Iraq and Iran, petroleum can combine with other economic assets—water and topsoil—to generate balanced agricultural and some industrial development. But the most essential single characteristic of industrial society—a skilled and trained population that serves as producers and consumers—is available precisely in the countries without petroleum deposits —Lebanon, Turkey, Egypt, and especially Israel—and it is here that a genuine process of industrialization has begun.

Social Foundations

Languages and Religions

Language and religion, in the Middle East as elsewhere, form the main basis for, as well as the main barrier to, national integration. Its peoples have often been said to form a linguistic and religious mosaic. Yet the heterogeneity of the region is not nearly as great or ingrained as such a statement would suggest. The major religious and linguistic divisions coincide with political boundaries, and some of the more picturesque minority groups are numerically small enough to be of greater interest to the historian than to the political and social scientist.

The main languages of the area are Arabic, Persian, and Turkish; Turkish being the national language of Turkey, Persian of Iran and Afghanistan, and Arabic of all the other countries except Israel. Of these, Arabic belongs to the Semitic family of languages, Persian to the Indo-Iranian branch of the Indo-European family, and Turkish to the Turkic branch of the Ural-Altaic family. Yet over the centuries there has been extensive borrowing of vocabulary and even grammatical forms from Arabic to Persian and from Arabic and Persian to Turkish. (Turkish was until 1928, and Persian is to this day, written in the Arabic script.) Other languages of the area include, in approximate order of numerical importance:

Pushtu (or Pashto), an Indo-Iranian language spoken by about half the population of Afghanistan, where it is the second official language.

Kurdish, an Indo-Iranian language spoken by the mountain population in the Iranian-Iraqi-Turkish border area.

A number of *Turkic* languages and dialects spoken in parts of Iran (Azeri, Qashqai, Turkmen) and Afghanistan (Uzbek).

A number of *Iranian* dialects prevalent in other parts of Iran (Baluchi, Bakhtiari, Lur, etc.) and Afghanistan (Tajik, Hazara).

Hebrew, a Semitic language revived as the language of Jewish immigrants in Palestine and the official language of Israel.

Armenian, an Indo-European language with an alphabetic script of its own spoken by a population once centered in northeastern Turkey but today surviving chiefly in the urban centers of Syria, Lebanon, and Iran (as well as the Soviet Union).

The religious picture is somewhat simpler. Islam is the faith of well over nine-tenths of the Middle Eastern population, and over two-thirds belong to the *Sunni,* or orthodox, branch of Islam. Their name derives from the Arabic word *sunnah,* meaning established practice, because they consider themselves bound to emulate where possible the practice of the Prophet and of the early Muslim community as recorded in the classics. All Sunnis, if they are sufficiently devout and affluent, try to make the prescribed pilgrimage to Mecca at least once in a lifetime (and after doing so take the honorific title *Hajj,* or Pilgrim). The major center of Sunni learning is the school, or university, attached to the Azhar mosque in Cairo. From a theological point of view, Sunnis may be divided into several "schools," among which the Maliki, Shafi, Hanafi, and Hanbali are the most prevalent. These differ mainly in minor points of ritual observance and legal doctrine, but respect each other as orthodox, go to the same mosques, and hence form a single religious community.

The most important among the non-Sunni denominations are the heterodox Muslims, known collectively as the *Shiah* (or more fully, as *Shiat Ali,* or "Faction of Ali"), because of their belief that the caliphate—that is, the succession to Muhammad in his capacity as leader of the faithful—should have been passed not through election but in the direct line of descent from the Prophet Muhammad through his cousin and son-in-law Ali and Ali's sons Hasan and Husayn. Perhaps 10 to 15 per cent of the approximately 400 million Muslims in the world belong to this group, most commonly known as *Shiis* or less frequently as *Alawis* (adjectives derived respectively from *Shiah* and from *Ali*). They observe a number of holidays ignored by the Sunnis, such as the anniversaries of the deaths of Ali and Husayn, go on pilgrimage to such Shii shrines as Karbala in Iraq and Mashhad in Iran, and generally accord greater authority to their ulama (commonly known as *mullahs* or, in the higher grades, as *mujtahids*) than do the Sunnis.

Much like Protestant Christianity, the Shiah is in turn divided into a number of rival sects, the most prominent of whom are the *Ja'fari* (or Twelver) Shiis, who believe that the twelfth descendant of Ali, a certain Ja'far, is the Hidden Imam (or Caliph) who will reappear on Judgment Day. The Shiis of Iran and of Iraq are Ja'faris. The other main branch of the Shiah are the *Ismailis* or Seveners, who hold that Ismail, the seventh Shii Caliph, is the Hidden Imam. They are numerous in Pakistan and East Africa and also in Syria, where they are known as *Alawis* or *Alaouites.* (Other Alawis form a prominent minority in Turkey, where however the reticence of Sunni government officials to recognize any schisms among Muslims has prevented any certain knowledge of their exact numbers, habits, or beliefs.)

The Ismailis are probably the best-known of Muslim sects among Westerners. Their contemporary habit of annual donations of gold and platinum to their head, known as the Aga Khan, makes an unforgettable impression on readers of the illustrated press. Centuries earlier, a group of Ismailis who consumed liberal doses of *hashish* and ambushed large numbers of Frankish Crusaders, became known to the latter as Assassins (from Arabic *hashishin*). A third group of Shiis are the *Zaydis,* who trace the correct caliphal line through a different branch of the Prophet's family, started by his great-grandson Zayd, directly to the royal house of Yemen, who therefore claim the title of Imam. Until the civil war of 1962–66, the Zaydis were the dominant minority in Yemen, although the Sunnis have always been a numerical majority.

There are about 4 million *Christians* in the Middle East. These form about half the population of Lebanon and important minorities among the Arab population of Syria, Jordan, and Israel; smaller Christian communities exist in the towns of Iraq, Iran, and Turkey, and in Egypt. These Christians are divided among a number of independent churches, such as the Copts (Egypt), the Maronites (Lebanon), the Syrian Christians, the Greek Orthodox (mainly in Turkey, Lebanon, and Syria), the Greek Catholics, the Gregorians (Armenians), and the Assyrians (Iraq and Iran). Except for many of the Armenians and for the Greeks of Turkey, all these Christian denominations speak the language of their native countries—i.e., Arabic or Persian.

Jews form the vast majority of the population of Israel, and the scattered Jewish communities of Iraq, Yemen, and Iran have in the past decade generally emigrated to that country.

The *Bahais* (mostly Persian speaking) are a nineteenth-century offshoot from Iranian Islam. The perhaps 400,000 Iranian Bahais are the only religious group subject to periodic harassment there. (Islam, considering itself the ultimate revelation, is far more tolerant of preceding religions such as Judaism and Christianity than of succeeding splinter groups.) The Bahais have a worldwide missionary activity and have their headquarters in Acre, Israel.

The *Druzes* (Arabic speaking) are a medieval offshoot from Shii Islam with a secret ritual of successive degrees of initiation. They escaped persecution largely by settling in the more inaccessible mountain areas of Lebanon and Syria. Groups of even lesser numerical significance include the *Zoroastrians*, adherents of the pre-Islamic religion of Iran, known in India as Parsis; the *Mandaeans*, followers of John the Baptist, who live in the towns of Iraq; and the *Yazidis*, a Kurdish-speaking group in the northern Iraqi mountains, who hold the principles of Good and Evil to be of equal religious dignity, and hence are erroneously known to their neighbors as "devil-worshipers."

The survival of so many languages and faiths in close compass is due to a number of distinct historical factors. The Middle East's geographic location has made it a passageway for migrations from adjoining world regions, and most of these migrations have left their linguistic residue. The region itself has since early historic times been a seedbed for the emrgence of religious faiths. The dynastic structure of Middle Eastern empires down to the Ottoman Empire has permitted the survival and geographic intermixture of many linguistic groups, and the tolerant attitude of Islam toward other revealed religions has aided the survival of a large variety of denominations.

To form an idea of the effect of religious and linguistic divisions on national integration, it is necessary to combine the data on language and religion, as has been done in Table 3-2. (Note that the percentage figures are necessarily approximate, since census data are inadequate in most countries and altogether lacking in some.) It will be seen that about half of the countries of the Middle East (Saudi Arabia, Jordan, Turkey, Syria, Egypt) are ethnically highly homogeneous, with at least nine-tenths of the population speaking the same language and belonging to the same religious denomination; and that only in one country does more than one-tenth of the population differ from the majority in both lan-

TABLE 3-2

LINGUISTIC AND RELIGIOUS COMPOSITION OF THE MIDDLE EAST [a]

Country	Percentage of population belonging to dominant: language or religion	Percentage of population belonging to dominant: language and religion	Percentage of population differing from majority in: either language or religion	Percentage of population differing from majority in: both language and religion
Saudi Arabia	100 Arabs	98 Arab Sunnis	2 Arab Shiis	—
Jordan	100 Arabs	94 Arab Sunnis	6 Arab Christians	—
Turkey	99 Muslims	91 Turkish Muslims	6 Kurdish Muslims 3 Arab Muslims	1 Greeks, Armenians, and Jews
Egypt	99 Arabs or Sunnis	91 Arab Sunnis	8 Arab Christians	—
Syria	97 Arabs or Sunnis	68 Arab Sunnis	13 Arab Christians 12 Arab Shiis 4 Kurdish Sunnis	3 Armenian Christians
Iran	88 Shiis	67 Persian Shiis	15 Turkish Shiis 3 Arab Shiis 2 Persian Bahais	4 Kurdish Sunnis
Yemen	100 Arabs	55 Arab Shiis	45 Arab Sunnis	—
Israel	89 Jews	54 Hebrew Jews	10 Yiddish Jews 3 Arab Jews	7 Arab Muslims 2 Arab Christians
Iraq	100 Arabs or Sunnis	50 Arab Shiis	30 Arab Sunnis 16 Kurdish Sunnis 3 Arab Christians	—
Afghanistan	70 Sunnis	50–60 Pushtu Sunnis	5–10 Uzbek Sunnis	30 Tajik Shiis
Lebanon	94 Arabs	30 Arab Maronites	20 Arab Sunnis 18 Arab Shiis 19 Arabs of various Christian denominations	6 Armenian Christians
			6 Arab Druzes	

[a] Figures are in most cases only very rough estimates. Afghanistan, Saudi Arabia, and Yemen have never taken a census. Turkey is the only country which has current census data on linguistic and religious composition.

guage and religion. None of the countries of the Middle East, therefore, has the ingrained ethnic cleavages that complicate the politics of Ceylon, or Malaya, or even India.

The groups that stand out most distinctly are those that differ from the majority in both language and religion. These include the Arab Muslims and Christians of Israel and the non-Muslim minorities (Greeks, Armenians, and Jews) in the large cities of Turkey. Of both these minority groups it is true that, regardless of their legal status, they have not so far been, and are not likely to be in the foreseeable future, socially accepted as full-fledged first-class citizens. Despite the official secularism of Turkey, adherence to Islam is still in practice considered a prerequisite of Turkish nationality. By contrast, a Muslim Kurd or Arab of southern or southeastern Turkey only needs to acquire a fluent command of the language to be accepted, for most purposes, as a Turk. The same is true, by and large, of Armenians in Syria and Lebanon; since there are sizable groups of Arab Christians in these countries, they can assimilate without great difficulty. Afghanistan has the most divided population of the Middle East, and as the transition from traditional monarchy to popular political participation proceeds, a sharpening of ethnic and denominational conflict may be anticipated.

The status of the Arabs in Israel even before 1967 was complicated by the fact that the State of Israel was specifically founded as a fulfillment of Zionist aspirations to create a political homeland for Jews from all countries—a rationale for state-founding which automatically excludes non-Jews from full membership. On the other hand, the Israeli constitutional and legal system includes elaborate guarantees of minority rights for the Arabs (thus Arabic is the language of the of the courts in the Arab-speaking parts of the country and the second official language in the Israeli Parliament); in addition, the economic opportunities opened up by Israel's rapid agricultural and industrial development, which contrast sharply with the misery of Arab refugees in neighboring countries, have tended to reconcile the Israeli Arabs to their situation.

The war of June 1967 established Israeli control over Old Jerusalem, the West Bank of Jordan, the Golan heights of Syria, the Gaza Strip, and the Sinai Peninsula. Despite the flight of a large number of Arabs to the eastern part of Jordan, this placed under Israeli control a population that is roughly one-third Arab and two-thirds Jewish, with higher birthrates among the Arabs likely to change the ratio in their favor. The 1967 *de facto* boundaries thus confronted Israeli leaders with a long-run dilemma: whether to preserve the Jewish national character of their state by denying full civic rights to the occupied Arabs, or whether to preserve the egalitarian character of their society by granting such rights.

Other minorities in the Middle East differ from the dominant group of their country only in either language or religion. A few words should be said about each of the countries where these minorities are of appreciable size.

In Iran, only about two-thirds of the population belong to the dominant Persian-speaking Shii group. These people live mainly in the central plateau, whereas the peripheral areas are inhabited (counterclockwise from the northwest) by the Azeri Turks (in Azerbayjan), by the Kurds, Lurs, Bakhtiaris, and Qashqais in the southwestern mountains, the Arabs along the Persian Gulf, the Baluchis in the southeast, and the Afghans and Turkmen in the northeast.

The vast majority of these minorities, however, are Shiis, although they speak their distinct Turkic (Azeri, Qashqai, Turkmen) or Indo-Iranian (Lur, Bakhtiari, Baluchi, etc.) languages. Persian for most of them is the language of literature and higher culture. The separatist movements in Azarbayjan and Persian Kurdistan after the Second World War would hardly have become as prominent as they did without the active instigation of organized Communists or without the presence of Soviet troops in that portion of the country.

In Israel, the figures for the linguistic composition of the country only reflect a temporary state of affairs. The vast majority of the population consists of immigrants or children of immigrants who—much like immigrants to the United States, but perhaps with even greater emotional fervor—expect to make major adjustments in adapting to and helping to build up their new country. The revival of Hebrew as the common language of the Jewish population of Israel has been an essential part of that process of adaptation and construction, and it is actively furthered both by government policy and by social pressure. Immigrants of the older generation continue to speak their native Yiddish, Arabic, Hungarian, Russian, etc., in private and get along as best they can with Hebrew in public; their children, however, will take considerable pride in speaking Hebrew exclusively. Hence the trend in Israel is definitely toward linguistic uniformity.

The religious and linguistic divisions of Afghanistan are greatly reinforced by the relative isolation of tribal and village communities in the large and small mountain valleys. Although Pushtu, Tajik, and Hazara are the major spoken languages, Persian (to which the first two are related) continues as the language of the court, of politics, and of literature. Whether this distinction between upper-class language and lower-class regional vernacular will survive a future process of social mobilization seems doubtful.

Iraq is almost evenly divided between Shiis and Sunnis, the Sunnis including a larger number of Arabic speakers and a smaller number of Kurds. Although the Kurds inhabit a distinct region in the north, the main distinction among the three groups is a social rather than a geographic one. The traditional upper class —landowners, urban intellectuals, and bureaucrats—consists predominantly of Sunni Arabs; the majority of the tenant farmers of the Euphrates-Tigris Valley are Shiis and the Kurds are tribal nomads in the mountain valleys of the north.

The only country of the Middle East which can appropriately be described as a "mosaic" is Lebanon, and indeed the country's political structure has long been based on an elaborate religious pluralism. The last denominational census, in 1932, listed 10 different Christian sects as well as Sunni and Shii Muslims, Druzes, Jews, and "others." The three largest of these 14 groups—the Maronite Christians, Sunni Muslims, and Shii Muslims—accounted for 30, 20, and 18 per cent of the population, respectively. There is much evidence that the proportion of Christians to Muslims and Druzes, which then was 55 to 44 per cent, has shifted in favor of the Muslims (mainly because of the higher Muslim birthrate). Yet the traditional formula of apportionment of legislative and executive power has been so thoroughly entrenched that any move to conduct a new census has been defeated. It should be remembered, however, that nearly all Lebanese speak Arabic as their native language, and that they share in the pragmatic-commercial spirit of a small country in whose economy transit trade, banking, and tourism play a predominant role. The most important single issue which tends to divide the Christians and Muslims is that of Lebanese vs. Pan-Arab nationalism, implying as it does a militant stance toward Israel. This issue plunged the country into a brief civil war at the height of Nasser's drive for Arab unity. A decade later it was the independent military action against Israel by armed Palestinian refugees that caused a similar strain.

Social Structure

The social structure of Middle Eastern peoples is not easily described in a few brief phrases. Differences of climate and economic habitat, of language and religion, and of historical experience contribute to the diversity of the picture. Even more crucial is the transformation brought about by the impact of Western civilization on the Islamic culture of the Middle East. In fact, the region's social character is best viewed as the intermingling in varying proportions of two distinct social systems—a traditional and a modern one.

The traditional social system of the Middle East has always been extremely status conscious. A man's social position, as well as his nationality, religion, and even occupation, were visible from afar by his dress and headgear, and any passerby would regulate his behavior accordingly. In Persian and Ottoman Turkish, forms of speech were carefully modulated according to the comparative rank of the interlocutors. The socioeconomic structure of the traditional Middle East was tripartite, with clearly distinct subcultures and styles of life prevailing in the towns, the villages, and the nomadic tribes.

The villages, from time immemorial, have included the vast majority of the region's population. The traditional village consists of a cluster of huts built from sunbaked brick of mud or clay, with stables below and two or three rooms for the peasant's family and for visitors above. The pale ochre of the huts would blend imperceptibly with the sunparched landscape, and the village would generally be at a safe distance from the main highways which might carry invading armies or such undesirable emissaries of central authority as tax collectors or conscription officers. Politically, the village thus would represent a self-contained microcosm, just as subsistence farming made it, by and large, economically self-sufficient.

Culturally, too, each village would be homogeneous. Turkish, Armenian, and Greek villages might alternate in close juxtaposition in Anatolia, and Maronite, Druze, and Sunni villages in the Lebanese mountains; but within each village a single language and denomination encompassed the entire population. Social rank within the village would depend largely on the size of a family's land holdings, with tenant farmers or day laborers forming a rural proletariat. The important office of village headman, although not nominally hereditary, was in fact restricted to members of the one or two wealthiest families. Aside from the headman, the local imam (or priest in a Christian village) would play a prominent role, although pagan beliefs and practices would often survive for centuries under the official veneer of monotheism. Disputes within the village would be settled according to local custom by the headman and the other village elders. Disputes with neighboring villages were frequent and endemic—set off when the herds of one village would stray on grazing land claimed by another, or when a boy from one village abducted a girl from the next—and would be fought out in pitched battles in the hills and perpetuated in blood feuds for generations to come.

The towns and cities of the traditional Middle East were the centers of commerce and manufacture, of government and learning, and of a fair degree of social mobility. In small and middling towns, especially in the Fertile Crescent and southern Turkey, patrician families held positions of well-entrenched local power and prestige—families such as the Cenanis in Ayintab (today Gaziantep), the Mardinizades in Mardin, the Gaylanis and Pachachis in Baghdad, the Umaris in Mosul, and the Nashashibis and Husaynis in Jerusalem. Many of these traced their descent to the time of the Crusades, and beyond that to the lineage of the Prophet Muhammad. Their power was based on large holdings of land in the environs of the town, often administered as family endowments, or on hereditary office, religious or secular.

While the patricians would represent the dominant religion—Sunni Islam in the Turkish and Arabic parts and the Shiah in Iran—the merchants and craftsmen of the towns, each branch organized in its separate guild, would include a liberal sprinkling of Armenians, Greeks, Jews, and other minorities. The largest urban centers—Istanbul in Turkey, Cairo in Egypt, and Tehran in Iran—included the elaborate machinery of central government: the palaces of sultan, shah, and princes of the blood; the mansions of vezirs, pashas, and other civil and military dignitaries; the large mosques with their libraries and *madrasahs* (or academies of Muslim learning); and the bazaars and quarters or streets reserved to the various trades—coppersmiths, jewelers, spicers, clothiers, cobblers, and the rest.

The nomadic tribes formed a set of autonomous units at the geographic and cultural periphery of Middle Eastern society. Their habitat in the mountains, steppes, and desert fringes was precarious. Their twice-yearly treks, from summer pasture in the mountain slopes to winter pasture in the valleys or from verdant steppe in the rainy season to desert oasis in the drought period, made heavy demands on organizational skill and experienced knowledge of terrain. Both the ever-present danger of raids by other tribes and the temptation of raiding them or the sedentary villages and towns fostered martial virtues. For all these reasons, a strict patriarchal organization prevailed among the nomads, with leadership firmly lodged in the shaykh of the head clan of each tribe, and within the chief tribe of each tribal confederation.

Needless to say, the authority of judge or tax collector in the nearby town, and of sultan or shah in the distant capital city was neither felt nor tolerated among the mountain and desert tribes. Appropriately, their roaming areas came to be known to their sedentary neighbors as the "Land of Insolence." The Ottoman sultans, who claimed suzerainty over the entire Arabian peninsula, would in fact do little more than play off one tribal confederation against another. Much the same technique was followed by Riza Shah of Iran (1925–41) who exiled the leaders of the powerful Qashqai confederation but allied his house in marriage to the rival Bakhtiaris—or for that matter by British agents operating from India or Egypt who gave liberal subsidies now to the Sharif of Mecca, now to Ibn Saud, and consistently to the shaykhs of the oil-rich Persian Gulf.

In all three subcultures of the traditional Middle East, the family structure is that of the patriarchal, patrilineal, patrilocal [1] extended family. Respect for age is considered one of the prime virtues, and indeed the title *shaykh*—claimed alike by the leaders of the tribes, the graduates of the Muslim theological university, al-Azhar, in Cairo, and by the abbots of dervish monasteries—simply means "old man." Subjection and seclusion of women are other widespread and characteristic Middle Eastern-Islamic traits, although in this respect there is a marked difference among city, village, and tribe. The veiling of women in public and their seclusion in separate parts of the house, known as *harem* (as distinct from the male *selâmlik*), was an urban and mainly an upper-class custom. Village women, working hard in the fields, can ill afford to cover their faces, and in the cramped quarters of the village mud hut with up to a half dozen family members of all sexes and generations sharing a room, the distinction between *harem* and *selâmlik* vanishes. And nomadic camp life encourages a freer mingling of adolescent girls and boys than obtains in either village or city. Similarly, by social custom, demographic arithmetic, and economic necessity, the practice of polygyny (one man marrying several wives—up to four being permitted by the Qur'an) was largely limited to the wealthier peasantry.

While social distinctions were explicit and steep, the traditional structure was by no means static or rigid. Islam, like Christianity, teaches the universal brotherhood of man, and thus affords no ideological justification of elaborate caste distinctions such as prevail in Hinduism. In contrast to Europe, moreover, the Islamic Middle East never developed a hereditary aristocracy with accredited political privileges. Landed property, passing from father to son, might give a family wealth and local influence for generations. (Such hereditary landownership was of particular importance in Egypt where large estates were held by an ethnically distinct caste, the Mamluks.) Descent from the Prophet gave title to the honorifics of Sharif or Sayyid and was carefully recorded by appropriate officials. Religious and secular office, such as that of *mufti* (jurisconsult), *qadi* (judge), or governor might in fact become hereditary for several generations. Yet the sociopolitical system provided several important correctives against any tendency toward hereditary power. The intricate rules of Muslim inheritance (in both the male and female lines) would quickly scatter any landed estates unless vested in indivisible family endowments. While governmental office would provide the opportunity for rapid accumulation of wealth, the treasury's practice of arbitrary confiscation soon would redress the balance. Autocracy, in the Middle East as in seventeenth- and eighteenth-century Europe, had a profoundly leveling influence, and in the Middle East most of the governmental tradition was purely autocratic without any interval or substratum of feudalism.

The Ottoman sultans, for example, recruited their military and civilian officials by preference from among prisoners of war and others whose technical status was that of slaves, precisely so as to prevent the rise of a self-reliant aristocratic class. Thus the military elite of the Ottoman Empire, the Janissaries, were originally drawn from among Christian boys levied as tribute from Balkan subjects; for several centuries they were forbidden to marry so as to prevent any temptation of nepotism or heredity. The military elite of Egypt, from the twelfth to the nineteenth centuries, was steadily replenished through the slave

[1] Anthropologist's term meaning (a family) taking up residence in the husband's location.

trade from among Turkic and Circassian tribes of the north Caucasus; their very name, Mamluks, is one of the Arabic words for "slave." Similarly, most of the Ottoman grand vezirs, down to the nineteenth century, were men of low birth and predominantly of non-Turkish and often even non-Muslim background.

Particularly in its period of greatest power, from the fifteenth to the eighteenth century, the empire attracted many able converts from Europe who rose rapidly in the military and civilian hierarchies. Only in times of imperial decay did something of an independent agrarian aristocracy assert itself, such as the *derebeyis*, or valley lords, who constituted a major challenge to the centralizing tendencies of Sultan Mahmud II (1808–39). Conversely, any young man of lowly origin who, by his own energy, through his parents' sacrifice, or through powerful protectors, had entered a *madrasah* or one of the military training schools could rise to the rank of mufti, qadi, or pasha without any stigma attaching to his antecedents. The sharp gradations of the social pyramid thus were smoothed over by a process of mobility, a mobility based not perhaps on equal opportunity but at least on equal chance.

The impact of modernity has brought about some very fundamental changes in this old social structure. The importance of the nomadic tribes has steadily declined. In part, they have been victims of technological obsolescence. Jeep, airplane, and pipeline have replaced the camel as vehicles for desert transportation, and hence the camel-herding nomads on the desert fringes have declined in numbers, wealth, and activity. Better irrigation has encouraged sheep and camel herders to settle down to till the soil. And industry, such as petroleum extraction and refining, with its many ancillary activities in the al-Hasa region of Saudi Arabia, has provided employment in towns.

Above all, the nomads are beginning to lose their age-old contest with central government. In the early twentieth century, nomadic tribes were prominent in the fight against establishment of foreign rule, or indeed of any solid governmental authority. The tribes of the Middle Euphrates challenged the imposition of British rule in Iraq in a widespread rebellion in 1921, and a few years later the Druze mountaineers south of Damascus set off an anti-French revolt that quickly spread to the rest of Syria, just as in Arab North Africa, the Berber tribes (or Kabyles, from Arabic *qabilah*) provided the focus of resistance to Spanish and French rule in Morocco and the Sanusi-led Cyrenaican tribes to Italian rule in Libya. The Kurdish tribes of eastern Turkey, following religious leaders of the Naqshbandi dervish order, strenuously opposed the establishment of the secular and nationalist Turkish Republic in 1925, and there was further unrest and violence in Turkish Kurdistan as well as in neighboring Iran and Iraq in the 1930s. During the same period, Riza Shah's government, almost for the first time in human memory, began to bring the tribes of southern Iran under the sway of the capital. Although these last manifestations of nomadic power provided some bitter and colorful encounters, the tribes' political position has never recovered from these blows; and changes in the economic habitat, especially "sedentarization," are likely to clinch the effect of these political changes.

More recently, with the turbulent transition from the Iraqi monarchy to various military regimes, which began in 1958, the Kurdish mountain warriors of the Sulaymaniyyah region have reasserted their independence. Although they have produced, under Mullah Mustafa al-Barzani, an unprecedented degree of intertribal unity, it seems doubtful that their size, organization, and natural resources are sufficient to permit the establishment of full-fledged nationality. In any purely military contest, Barzani's forces have been able to hold their own against vastly superior numbers of the regular forces. Yet they are in no position, without assistance of outside military power, to inflict any decisive defeat on the central government. The airplane has not only made the camel obsolete for transportation in the desert; it also has placed the highland nomad on the defensive in his mountain fastness.

The village remains the stronghold of Middle Eastern traditionalism, but here, too, changes are felt. Technological innovations, such as perennial irrigation of the Nile Valley since the turn of the century, the development of a railroad system throughout the Middle East in the decades before the First World War, and, above all, the rapid expansion of highway networks since the 1940s have made it possible for villagers to produce cash crops for distant markets. With trade have come new ideas and modes of living. Governments have built waterwells and elementary schools. Enterprising villagers have opened coffee houses, barbershops, and groceries, and recruits returning from military duty have used their newly learned mechanical skills to operate garages and service stations. The programs of the government-owned radio station (broadcast full blast from a loudspeaker suspended from a tree crotch in front of the new coffee house or picked up on portable transistor sets) give even the illiterate villager much the same exposure to world news—and to government propaganda —as his city cousin. Migration to the cities usually comes in stages: the villager first goes into town in search of occasional employment as construction worker, porter, or handyman; then he begins to work in town steadily but returns to his village at harvest time, or at least for family weddings or to settle some title deed; he is likely to bring his bride to the town from his native village, too, and later on his children will begin to grow up as townspeople.

It is in the urban Middle East that the most dynamic changes have taken place. Here a modernized educated elite has grown up, including lawyers, doctors, engineers, merchants, journalists, and army officers. The most numerous category within the ruling class is that of government administrator. For, in a setting where private initiative is at a premium, even the professions of law, medicine, and engineering find their most secure employment in government agencies. All of these city residents are thoroughly Western in their tastes— whether it be the pin-stripe suit of the businessman; the Parisian decolleté of the socialite matron; the blue jeans, chewing gum, and jazz records of the teen-ager; the radio, tape recorder, and sports car of the conspicuous consumer; or the highbrow intellectual's subscription to the *New Statesman and Nation*.

The revolution which has created this new upper class was, above all, an educational revolution, and it has been so thoroughgoing because it dates back a hundred years or more. Indeed, of all the multifarious reforms attempted in the nineteenth century, the establishment of schools and colleges by Europeans and Americans, and by Middle Easterners emulating European and American models, has been the most effective and lasting one. Institutions such as the American University of Beirut and Victoria College in Alexandria were the first places where, toward the turn of the century, Arab Muslims mingled freely with Arab Christians of various religious denominations, and thus came to develop a common Arab consciousness. It was the predecessor of the American University of Beirut, as we noted in an earlier context, which introduced the first Arab printing press to Lebanon in its efforts to supply the need for modern textbooks for its students. Constantinople College (now called American College for Girls) long was, in effect, restricted to Christian students. But its first Muslim graduate, Halide Edib, achieved worldwide fame as a novelist and playwright.

Today even more than in traditional times, education is the major highway of social mobility. The junior high school years are likely to prove crucial. If a peasant family can manage to send its son to the nearest town to complete such a school, he can thenceforth make his career by his own wits and application, by entering a university on one of the meager but highly coveted state scholarships and rising in the profession of his choice. For many members of this educational elite, the basic Westernized training received in Middle Eastern schools is supplemented by further study in Europe or in the United States. Thus Iran and Turkey today send more university students abroad than almost any other country of their size.

The Westernized educated class of the Middle East is heavily clustered in the capitals and other large cities: Beirut, Cairo, Alexandria, Istanbul, Ankara, Izmir, Aleppo, Damascus, Tehran, Baghdad. Only a sprinkling, conversely, will be found in towns with less than 50,000 inhabitants. University graduates, it is true, will find themselves assigned as district officers, government doctors, or judges to small towns throughout their country. But such service in the provinces is considered a form of exile, a necessary if unpleasant apprenticeship to be endured at the beginning of a career. The aspiring young intellectual will therefore employ his diligence, ingenuity, and connections in high places to rise at the earliest opportunity to a more fitting position in one of the ministries or elsewhere in the capital.

The possibility of access from the peasantry into the ruling class, therefore, in no way serves to blur the sharp distinction between upper and lower class or to lessen the status consciousness of those on either side of the barrier. In contrast to the peasant turned construction worker, who continues to commute between town and village, the village-born member of the Middle Eastern elite is notoriously eager to leave his peasant antecedents far behind. He is more likely to travel to London, Moscow, or San Francisco than to journey extensively in the rural districts of his own country; to bring his aged parents into town than to return to his native village for more than the briefest visit. If anything, the gulf between the urban upper class and the peasantry today is more pronounced than it used to be. What once was solely a *social* difference within a relatively homogeneous Muslim-Middle Eastern context, today has also become a *cultural* gulf between traditional villager and Westernized intellectual.

Aside from the urban upper class and the peasantry, there is a third social group in the contemporary Middle East which, for the sake of simplicity, we may call the urban lower class. This is a highly varied stratum. It includes the coppersmith on the steep cobblestone alley who tinkers his immemorial rhythm in his open shop; the *muezzin* who from his minaret perch praises God and calls the faithful to prayer five times a day; the obsequious salesclerk in the haberdashery store; the taxidriver who with skillful abandon bounces through the scrambled traffic at breakneck speed; the operators of the humming textile mill; the corner grocer amid his tincans and bags of flour and dried beans; the brick-layer atop the scaffolding which will unveil a luxury apartment house; a veritable army of janitors, handymen, maids, and laundresses who perform the domestic chores of the rich; and an even larger number of unemployed whom rural over-population and elusive urban opportunity have driven into town.

But there is one thing all these colorful, characteristic figures have in common. Whether they are recent migrants from the village or have been city dwellers for generations, they have been raised in a static, devout, traditional context and now find themselves in close contact with a Westernized, competitive, secularized setting of which they experience most of the frustrations and few of the rewards. It is this urban lower class, therefore, which provides the recruits for the organized fundamentalist movements such as the Muslim Brotherhood or the Nation party in Turkey. The same lower urban stratum, under the leadership of uprooted intellectuals, has supplied some of the membership of the Communist parties. In unorganized form, it furnishes the manpower for the recurrent street demonstrations, mob scenes, and riots which have become a ubiquitous ingredient of Middle Eastern political activity.

The traditional triad of townsman, villager, and tribesman thus has made way for the contemporary triad of urban upper class, urban lower class, and peasantry. The dynamism of the cultural and social scene that has created these new classes in the Middle East has also been reflected in profound changes in political ideology and the prevailing notions of legitimacy.

Chapter *4*

The Foundations of Politics
IDEOLOGY

Nationalism

Ask any hundred politically articulate Middle Easterners about their loyalty, their political ideals, their notions of legitimacy, and at least ninety-five will tell you that they are nationalists, dedicated to the power, glory, and well-being of their nation. This chorus in unison, moreover, is not the product of police-state coercion or long habituation under totalitarian rule: it is sincere and spontaneous. But several things are noteworthy about this near-unanimity.

First, it is restricted precisely to the politically articulate strata, i.e., mainly to the urban and educated groups. The masses of illiterate villagers, by contrast, have as yet little notion of nation, nationality, or nationalism. They are likely to reply to the stranger's query that they are Muslims, and that they come from such a village or such a district: their loyalties are to this day what Middle Eastern loyalties have been for centuries: religious and local. In part, therefore, the urban elite's fervor in professing its adherence to nationalism reflects the common struggle in which it finds itself engaged to educate the peasantry to active national consciousness.

Second, the ideal of the nation-state, so ubiquitously and loudly proclaimed today, came to the Middle East only very recently. The Turkish-speaking rulers of the pre-1918 empire were proud to call themselves Ottomans; their loyalty was ultimately defined by attachment to the house of Osman and to the supranational Islamic Middle Eastern culture which had been consolidated under six centuries of Ottoman imperial rule. Even the nineteenth-century political exiles, who among their European hosts were known as Young Turks, called them-

32

selves New Ottomans, adopting the Western term only as a French loanword, "Jön Türk." The cumulative defeats of the Libyan, Balkan, and World Wars (1911–18) gradually converted this Ottoman elite to a Turkish national consciousness. But Ziya Gökalp, poet and ideologist of the Young Turk Union and Progress party, still bracketed Turkification with Islamization and Modernization in his famous political pamphlet; and even Mustafa Kemal, later known as Atatürk or "Father of the Turks," at first had to disguise his nationalist aims behind a show of Ottoman-dynastic and Muslim-religious loyalty in the first years of his *de facto* government at Ankara (1920–23).

At that, the Turks were among the earliest devotees of nationalism in the Middle East. Arab nationalism had found some early intellectual precursors and spokesmen in the nineteenth century; but it did not become the creed of the educated elite in the Fertile Crescent until the centralizing Turkifying tendencies of the Union and Progress dictatorship (1913–18) rudely shattered earlier Ottoman dreams of "unity of the elements"—i.e., multinational harmony within the empire. The Egyptians, today the most vocal spokesmen of Pan-Arab nationalism, wavered between an Egyptian and a Pan-Arab identification as late as the 1920s and 1930s.

In Iran, the flowering of Persian language and literature during and after centuries of Arab and Mongol-Turkish conquest, and devotion to Shii Islam which emerged as the state religion in the sixteenth century, provided continuing points of attachment for patriotic feeling. But only the struggle against British and Russian encroachments and influence since the turn of the century, and especially since the Second World War, converted this patriotic tradition into a militant national consciousness. The case of Israel is even more striking. Zionism arose as an organized movement among European Jewry in the late nineteenth century. The Balfour Declaration of 1917 added the concrete promise of a "national home" in Palestine for which large-scale immigration since the 1920s and the proclamation of the State of Israel in 1948 laid a realistic basis.

Third, nationalism in the Middle East began as an ambivalent reaction to the recent European impact on the Middle East, ambivalent because it was compounded of opposition and imitation. Turkish nationalism arose largely in response to the militant nationalism of the Balkan Christian subjects of the Ottoman Empire, who were supported in their aspirations by the nationalist-imperialist powers of Europe. Another important contribution came from Turko-Tatar refugees from the Kazan, Azarbayjan, and Crimean regions of the late Czarist Empire, themselves propelled to national consciousness in reaction to the rise of Great Russian nationalism. And the impulse which came from the Balkans and Russia to Turkey was passed on, by the same chain reaction, to the Arabs to the southeast. After the First World War, the establishment of British and French mandates in the Fertile Crescent provided a logical target for nationalist attack, and since the Second World War the proclamation of the State of Israel has keenly aroused Arab nationalist sensitivities.

The same ambivalent mixture of admiration and hate that the ideologists of emerging nationalism display toward their external antagonists tends to characterize their attitude toward their own history. The immediate past is viewed with shame and horror as one of backwardness and oppression. By contrast, the image of a strong and glorious nation, which it is the nationalist's task and that permitted the garrisoning of British troops in Iraq, Jordan, and Egypt, or the establishment of American bases in Saudi Arabia; the departure of British and other European advisers; and the nationalization of such Western-owned assets as the Anglo-Iranian Oil and Suez Canal Companies. At a time when the remaining "imperialist" positions of privilege were British or American, the support of the Soviet Union and other Communist countries was warmly welcomed by Arab nationalists (just as some of their predecessors were tempted to intrigue with the Nazis against the British or indeed with the British against the Ottomans). The defeat of 1967 drove the Arab countries, and particularly Egypt and Syria, further into the Soviets' arms.

Monarchy vs. Republic

Aside from other ambiguities, nationalism gives no guidelines as to the legitimate internal form of government or the content of domestic policy. Nationalism implies the direct participation of all citizens within the common affairs of the nation; it therefore presents an egalitarian bias and also one toward representative government. But equality and representation may be achieved, approximated, or indeed simulated, through a variety of constitutional forms.

The major forms of government in the recent and contemporary Middle East have been monarchy (absolute or constitutional), parliamentary government, and a variety of dictatorships. The monarchic principle is firmly rooted in tradition and went unquestioned until the early twentieth century. Caliphs, sultans, shahs, khedives, and amirs, symbolized the same patriarchal authority visible in the nomadic shaykh, the village headman, or the head of any Middle Eastern family. And in all Middle Eastern states, except the earliest caliphate, monarchic succession had always been hereditary, though more often hereditary by seniority than by primogeniture. Hence the nineteenth- and early twentieth-century reformers aimed at curtailing the monarch's absolute powers rather than at abolishing monarchy as such.

The Ottoman Empire in 1876 and Iran in 1905–6 were the first and third Asian states (with Japan in 1889 intervening as the second) to adopt written constitutions in the European manner; a movement in Egypt aiming at constitutional limitation of monarchy was thwarted by the British occupation of 1882. Although monarchs in the political struggles of this period were frequently deposed (the Sultan, for example, in 1807, 1808, 1876 twice, and 1909,—i.e., five out of seven Ottoman rulers of the period) and at times assassinated, they were regularly replaced with princes of the same house. The Syrian Nationalist Congress of Damascus elected the Sharif Faysal king of Syria in 1920; under British aegis, monarchies were established in Iraq (1921, again under Faysal whom the French had ousted from Syria in the meantime), and Transjordan (1923 under Faysal's elder brother Abd Allah); and in Iran, Riza Khan, a former army sergeant who had seized power in a military coup in 1921, proclaimed himself shah in 1925 in lieu of the deposed Qajar dynasty.

Mustafa Kemal set a precedent of fundamental change when, following the deposition of Sultan Mehmed VI Vahideddin in 1922, he had Turkey declared a republic the following year. In Syria and Lebanon, republican constitutions were adopted in the interwar period, and under a French mandate these seemed just as natural as monarchical constitutions in British-mandated Iraq and Transjordan or in British-occupied Egypt. But this very association with foreign rule did much to discredit monarchy as such. Young nationalists came to be persuaded that monarchy facilitated the designs of European imperialists, since it required the foreign corruption or control of only a single individual at the head of the state. The Egyptian revolution of 1952 exiled the debauched King Faruq and, after a brief experiment with guardianship for his infant son, instituted a republic. The bloody Iraqi revolution of 1958 cost the lives of King Faysal II and his uncle, the ex-regent Abd al-Ilah, and once again a republic resulted.

In Jordan and Iran, monarchy since the 1950s has been precariously pitted against the surging forces of social unrest and political revolt. On one occasion, in 1953, the Shah of Iran already had hurried into exile when a countercoup under General Zahidi (said to have been backed by the U.S. Central Intelligence Agency) unexpectedly restored him to power. In Saudi Arabia, the steady impact of the oil industry on the socioeconomic structure of the population and the corrupting influence of oil royalties on the royal house and its entourage are beginning to wear down the puritanical foundations of the Wahhabi kingdom. In Yemen, bloody palace coups and assissinations of imams and princes had long been endemic. When Imam Ahmad, a cruel, disease-ridden autocrat, died in 1962, a military conspiracy overthrew his successor, Muhammad al-Badr, and a civil war between republican and monarchist forces resulted. In Afghanistan alone did monarchy, for the time being, seem secure.

But the formal change from monarchy to republic does not of itself mean an abandonment of the centralized personal direction of the affairs of state; on the contrary, it often means a tightening of such personal control in the hands of a popular dictator, such as Atatürk in Turkey (1923–38), or Nasser in Egypt (1954–   ), or less successful attempts in the same direction by various Syrian and Iraqi military leaders. Even where a representative competitive system of government was in operation for a time, personal rule soon reemerged—as in Turkey under Premier Adnan Menderes (1950–60).

Tradition vs. Change

The transition from monarchies to republics and personal dictatorships is one important indication of the transformation which has occurred in the ideological climate of the Middle East within the last generation. In the early part of this century, the chief ideological motivation of Middle Eastern statesmen and politicians was a self-conscious defense of inherited institutions and values against the crushing military, political, and cultural onslaught of the European West. A good deal of cultural borrowing from the West was in fact combined with this defensive posture. The Egyptian reforms of Muhammad Ali and the Turkish reforms of Mahmud II and his successors had introduced Western military discipline and equipment, and the Westernization of finance, administration, education, and even parts of the law followed in the course of a logical chain reaction.

Even Abdülhamid's Pan-Islamic policy—his claim to the caliphate as a spiritual overlordship over Islamic peoples outside the Ottoman imperial realm— was in fact patterned on Christian notions of separation of church and state and on corresponding claims of the papacy, rather than on authentic Islamic tradition. And the religious reforms of the turn of the century in Egypt, even while reasserting Islam in the purity of the early caliphal period, were adapting for their own use the weapons of European historical and scientific learning which they encountered in their polemics with European theologians. But the rationale for these borrowings was the desire to defeat the enemy by judicious use of his own weapons: the cultural climate was one of "defensive modernization," to use Cyril Black's term.[2]

The early Arab nationalist movement still largely falls within the same category. The Arab revolt of 1916 emanated from an alliance of the Bedouin warriors, led by the Sharif of Mecca and his sons, with the urban conspirators of Damascus and dissident Iraqi officers within the Ottoman army. The regimes established in the Fertile Crescent in the 1920s, particularly those in Iraq and Transjordan, respresented a consolidation of established interests of landed aristocrats and urban patricians under the leadership of monarchs whose credentials were of recent origin (though hollowed by claim of descent from the Prophet) but whose methods of rule had a traditional character.

The Ottoman revolution of 1908 for the first time brought a basic change in attitude. The leaders of the Macedonian rebellion that forced the reintroduction of the 1876 constitution were young officers in their late twenties and early thirties. After the military *coup d'état* of 1913, these men, operating through the Committee of Union and Progress, were no longer content to exercise power from behind the scenes; they stepped forward to assume active leadership of the affairs of state. Imperceptibly but rapidly their program shifted from one of defense of Ottoman traditions to an assertion of Turkish nationalism. Their political and social reform program was far more radical and comprehensive than anything that had preceded it during the previous century. The exploits of youth in the revolution of 1908 and the following years produced a heady sense of intoxication which was in sharp contrast with traditional Middle Eastern reverence for age and experience. In the broad contest between tradition and reform, the presumption no longer was in favor of maintenance of tradition, and change came to be accepted as a positive value in itself. The Kemalist revolution in Turkey only sanctioned in legal practice a transformation which the Young Turk period after 1908 had thoroughly prepared on the ideological-emotional level—the wholesale abandonment of political, legal, religious, and cultural traditions in favor of the very European institutions which earlier generations had so valiantly fought to resist.

The Arab revolutions in Egypt (1952) and in Iraq (1958), as well as the abortive Iranian revolution under Musaddiq (1951–53), brought a similar infusion of youth into the political scene and represented a similar acceptance of change—radical change—as a good in itself. Where the Turkish revolution of Kemal had been primarily political and cultural, these newer revolutionary movements concentrated on change in social and economic structure: land reform,

[2] *The Dynamics of Modernization* (New York: Harper & Row, Publishers, 1966).

rapid industrialization, a government-planned economy, an expansion of social welfare and security schemes. A nondoctrinaire and pragmatic socialism combined with nationalism as the dynamic ideology of the aspiring Middle Eastern masses and their political leaders.

Monism vs. Pluralism

The traditional social-political structure of Islamic countries combined a good deal of pluralism within a unitary overall structure of religion and state. The Christian and Jewish minority populations enjoyed a recognized judicial autonomy within the so-called *millet* system, and lack of transport and inefficiency of governmental machinery conferred a *de facto* autonomy on tribes, on local magnates, and even on individual villages. The centralizing absolutism of the nineteenth-century rulers established a far more effective unitary authority over their far-flung possessions. And the ideology of nationalism promoted an even more compact cohesion, which the general process of social mobilization, the increased role of the state within the economy, and the progress of party organization under populist dictatorships served to spread throughout the population. In most Middle Eastern countries, pluralist tendencies assert themselves only in the narrow confines of a landed oligarchy or else in the internal competition for power among several allied groups who jointly support a dictatorial single-party system, such as the army, bureaucracy, and professions in the Kemalist Republican People's party of the 1920s and 1930s; or the army, bureaucracy, labor groups, and the Ba'th party in Syria.

A more genuine and deepseated pluralism is to be found in Israel, Lebanon, and Turkey. In Israel, the tradition of proportional representation and coalition government (which originated within the Zionist representative institutions even before proclamation of the state), has engendered a party pluralism whereby not only positions in the bureaucracy are assigned to followers of various parties, but also several parallel school systems satisfy the demands of secularists and various shades of religious orthodoxy. In Lebanon, the basic pact which divides government positions (appointive and elective) proportionately among the various denominational groups has survived since mandate days; it was subjected to considerable strain in the civil war of 1958 which found Maronite advocates of Lebanese independence solidly aligned against Sunni Muslim sympathizers of Nasser's Pan-Arab program, but it reemerged as the only feasible formula of coexistence once civil order was restored. Turkey, finally, offers a rare example of deepening pluralism since its transition from a one-party to a multiparty system (1945–; cf. below, chap. 5).

Religion vs. Secularism

Traditional loyalties in the Middle East, as we have seen, were religious, dynastic, local, and tribal. But the advent of modern nationalism has brought about a profound change in the role and importance of religion. Mustafa Kemal in Turkey, after victory in the War of

Independence, abolished the caliphate, the dervish orders, and the traditional Islamic legal system. He undertook no separation of "church" and "state" on the Western model, the institution of a privately administered and financed religious organization being thoroughly alien to Islamic tradition and experience. Rather the religious institutions that remained (mosque officials, etc.) were downgraded in the government hierarchy and put in the charge of secularist officials.

In the Arab countries, there has been no correspondingly drastic break with religious tradition. The law codes in Syria and Egypt in the 1940s and 1950s did not simply transfer European models (as did Mustafa Kemal's "Turkish" civil and "Turkish" criminal codes which were replicas of Swiss and Italian models), but tried to codify Islamic precedent with suitable concessions to the demands of a modern age. Nasser also made great use of Islamic themes in his Pan-Arab propaganda; yet even a cursory reading of his *Philosophy of the Revolution* indicates the complete inversion of the traditional priority of values. Where traditional Middle Easterners felt themselves to be Muslims first and Arabs or Egyptians afterwards, Nasser glorifies Islam as a dynamic force for Arab unity, and puts both in the service of an Egyptian foreign policy. Significantly, he interprets the Islamic duty of pilgrimage to Mecca not as a religious ritual but as a device for the maintenance of political solidarity among Muslim countries.

But even in "secularist" Turkey, religion plays an unexpected residual role in the very definition of nationality, a role which, because of the ethnic composition of the country, is even more pronounced than in the less self-consciously "secularist" Arab states. All residents of Turkey—Turkish and Kurdish Muslims, Greek and Armenian Christians, and Jews—are equal in the eyes of the law and share the privileges of Turkish citizenship. When asked about his nationality, a member of the Turkish peasantry is as likely to indicate that he is a "Muslim" as that he is a "Turk." A Kurd, who is a Muslim in any case, can also become a Turk merely by acquiring an acceptable command of the language. By contrast, a Greek-speaking resident of Istanbul is accepted legally, and for some purposes socially, as a Turkish citizen. But both he and his Turkish-speaking fellow citizens would indignantly reject the notion that his nationality is "Turkish" rather than "Greek." The circumstance that the modern Turkish word for nation (*millet*) in Ottoman times denoted one of the autonomous religious communities of the empire both reflects and reinforces this conscious connection between religion and nationality. By contrast, a Syrian or Lebanese is an "Arab" by virtue of his language (and ancestral heritage), regardless of whether he is a Sunni or Shii Muslim or a Maronite, Syrian, or Greek Christian.

Islam as an ingredient of the definition of Turkish nationality or as a reinforcement of Pan-Arab aspirations—both represent a blending of religious motifs into the new nationalism. But this connection should not conceal the basic opposition of nationalist reform policies to the political traditions of Islam. Islam, both in its early history and in its later doctrine, was a polity as well as a religion. There is no equivalent in Qur'anic revelation of the Christian distinction of the things that are God's and the things that are Caesar's.[3] Muhammad was both prophet and founder of a state; his successors, the Caliphs, bore the

[3] For an elaboration of this point, see my chapter in Almond and Coleman, *Politics of the Developing Areas*, p. 379.

titles of *imam* (i.e., spiritual leader of the community) and *amir al-mu'minin* ("Commander of the Faithful"); the classical Muslim view of international affairs divides the world into the "House of Islam" and the "House of War"; and the body of Islamic doctrine, known as *fiqh* or *shariah* (and based on the Qur'an, sayings attributed to the Prophet, the practice of the early Muslim community, and interpretations by the classical theologians), encompasses in one seamless web what in the European tradition would be called theology, law, and ethics. In theory, this Islamic law was immutable, and the decrees of sultans or other rulers could only supplement but not amend or abrogate it.

In the light of this tradition of fusion of religion and public life, the modern nationalist's claim (most clearly formulated by the Turkish Kemalists) that he is not opposed to religion but will put it in its proper place as a matter of private conscience cuts as deeply at the root of Islamic tradition as does the formal enactment of European law codes in the place of the *shariah*. But even the more conservative reform of law as evidenced in recent codes in Syria, Egypt, and Tunisia departs drastically from Islamic precedent: where once religious law, all-engulfing in theory, made some grudging concessions to the ruler's secular power of decree, the modern codes, however "Islamic" their content, derive their validity from the enactment of secular parliaments.

The traditional Islamic fusion of religion and polity has survived in Afghanistan and, until recently, in Yemen (reinforced in the latter by the ruler's claim to lineal descent from the Prophet in the Alid line), and in Saudi Arabia. In other countries, Islamic-fundamentalist movements have grown up which militantly reassert presumed tenets of early Islamic tradition against the onslaught of secular nationalism and cultural Westernization. Such are the Muslim Brotherhood in Egypt and Syria, the Fidaiyan-i Islam (or Devotees of Islam) in Iran, and, to some extent, the Nation party and other dissident groups in Turkey. These combine their religious appeal with highly up-to-date methods of propaganda and mass organization, of social welfare services for their members, and in some cases of violence in waves of assassination, organized riots, and guerrilla warfare. They typically appeal to "those segments of the population which have been torn out of their traditional social context by urbanization and industrialization without having found a satisfactory place in the modern order of things." [4] Their strength will thus depend not on the force of tradition itself but rather on the success or failure of the social reform policies of their secularist rivals.

Communism

Much irrelevant speculation has been put into print about the supposed affinity or opposition between Islam and communism. Those arguing a close relationship between the two stress that both are bodies of doctrine demanding complete submission and obedience of the individual; those arguing opposition claim that Islamic morality in the Middle East is the surest bulwark against godless communism. Islam—like Christianity or any other ancient and complex body of revelation—can certainly be adapted

[4] Almond and Coleman, *Politics of the Developing Areas*, pp. 418ff.

to contemporary political issues in varying and contradictory ways. But the more important fact to remember is that communism as a doctrine appeals most strongly to segments of the urban intelligentsia, whereas Islam in its traditional form has its stronghold among the illiterate peasantry. The number of card-holding Communists is infinitesimally small—in the Arab countries it has recently been estimated at around 30,000. Russian experience itself indicates that such small groups may, in an unstable and revolutionary situation, wield a power quite disproportionate to their numbers. Nevertheless, Communist power seems far more likely to come to the Middle East today through foreign-policy alliances with nationalist regimes than through any domestic expansion of card-carrying Communist membership.[5]

[5] For a fuller discussion, see my eassay on "Communism and Islam," in J. Harris Proctor, ed., *Islam and International Relations* (New York: Frederick A. Praeger, Inc., 1965).

Chapter *5*

POLITICAL DYNAMICS

Three Major Patterns of Dynamics

✳ Any discussion of the political dynamics of the Middle East is complicated by two characteristic features of the region—its division into more than a dozen independent political entities, and the pervasive instability of political processes in most of these individual countries. Any adequate understanding of current political dynamics must rest therefore not only on an examination, as presented in the preceding chapters, of the history, geography, socioeconomic structure, and ideological setting of the region as a whole. It also must be reinforced and diversified by an examination of the particular circumstances which, in the lifetime of the present generation, have molded the political consciousness of statesmen, of party leaders, of spokesmen for organized interests, and of common citizens in each particular country.

Both the political division of the Middle East into its present diversity of sovereign states and the instability of political processes in many of the individual countries go back to the interplay, in the first half of the twentieth century, between the historical traditions of the region and the unsettling forces of modernization. In two of the countries—Turkey and Israel—intensive programs of modernization have been undertaken under indigenous leadership. In Turkey, the initial motivation was the desire to strengthen the social and political structure so as to ward off the threat of imperialist partition and colonial domination. In Israel, the large influx of immigrants from Europe during the Palestine mandate and their subsequent assertion of political independence within a hostile environment provided the incentive for the building of a dynamic modern society. At the other end of the spectrum stand Yemen and Afghanistan, which by virtue of their geographic remoteness long remained inaccessible to the forces of modernization. Only in our own day have the forces of competitive foreign assistance by Eastern and Western powers begun to undermine the traditional feudal and tribal agricultural and pastoral structure of politics and society.

In the other countries of the region, the seesaw struggle between forces of tradition and modernity has been most intense and hence the political situation most unstable. There are thus three distinct groups of countries represented in the Middle East each with their own patterns of political dynamics, and these may be labeled, for purposes of convenience, "modern political systems" (Turkey and Israel), "traditional political systems" (Yemen and Afghanistan), and "political systems in flux" (Egypt, Iran, Saudi Arabia, and the countries of the Arab Fertile Crescent). The following sections will briefly review the major dynamic features of each group and each country, starting with the most numerous group of "political systems in flux." Only against this background of dynamic variety will the subsequent regionwide discussion of parties, elections, and interest groups become meaningful (see Table 5-1).

TABLE 5-1

MIDDLE EASTERN REGIMES AND HEADS OF STATE

Afghanistan

Independent kingdom, constitutions adopted in 1931 and 1964.
    Amir Amanullah, 1919–1929 (declared king, 1926; forced to abdicate, 1929).
    Muhammad Nadir Shah, 1929–1933 (assassinated).
    Muhammad Zahir Shah, 1933–   .

Egypt (United Arab Republic)

Nominally part of the Ottoman Empire; from which it became independent *de facto* during the reign of Muhammad Ali (1805–1849). Rulers successively assume the titles of Pasha, Khedive (1867), Sultan (1914), and King (1922). British military occupation from 1882. Independence proclaimed 1922, but strong British influence continues until 1946. Monarchy overthrown in military coup of 1952. Union with Syria proclamied 1958 and dissolved 1961, but the official name United Arab Republic is retained.
    King Faruq, 1935–1952.
    General Muhammad Naguib, President of the Republic, 1952–1953.
    Colonel Gamal Abdul Nasser, President, 1954–   .

Iran

Independent monarchy; constitution adopted in 1905–1906.
Pahlavi dynasty, 1925–   .
    Shah Riza Pahlavi, 1925–1941, dictator since 1921 as Minister of War and Premier, exiled by Allies to South Africa.
    Shah Muhammad Riza Pahlavi, 1941–   , ruled with pseudo-parliamentary cabinets, briefly ousted in 1953 by Premier Muhammad Musaddiq, but quickly restored by General Fazlullah Zahidi.

Iraq

British mandate, 1920–1932.
Independent monarchy, 1932–1958, but close relations with British continued under treaty of 1930, later replaced by Baghdad Pact (1955–1958).

King Faysal I, 1921–1933.
King Ghazi, 1933–1939 (killed in automobile accident).
King Faysal II, 1939–1958; Regent Abd al-Ilah, 1939–1953 (both killed in revolution).
Republic (under successive military rulers), 1958–   .
    General Abd al-Karim Qasim, 1958–1963 (executed).
    Colonel Abd al-Salam Muhammad Arif, 1963–1966 (killed in accident).
    General Abd al-Rahman Muhammad Arif, 1966–1968 (deposed).
    General Hasan al-Bakr, 1968–   .

Israel

Proclaimed as independent state upon termination of British mandate over Palestine, May 15, 1948. Coalition governments led by Mapai party.
    Presidents: Chaim Weizmann, 1948–1952.
             Itzhak Ben-Zvi, 1952–1963.
             Shneor Zalman Shazar, 1963–   .
    Prime Ministers: David Ben Gurion, 1948–1953, 1955–1963.
             Moshe Sharett, 1953–1955.
             Levi Eshkol, 1953–1969.
             Golda Meir, 1969–   .

Jordan

Eastern part of British mandate over Palestine made into Amirate of Transjordan, 1921; proclaimed independent kingdom, 1946; enlarged by annexation of parts of Palestine, 1949, and renamed Hashimite Kingdom of Jordan.
    Amir (later King) Abd Allah, 1921–1951 (assassinated).
    King Tallal, 1951–1952 (declared insane).
    King Husayn, 1952 –   .

Kuwayt

Principality protected by United Kingdom under treaty of 1899, declared independent, 1961.
    Shaykh Abd Allah al-Salim al-Sabah, 1950–   .

Lebanon

Part of French mandate, 1920; proclaimed an independent republic, 1941; French occupation withdrawn, 1946.
    Presidents: Bisharah al-Khuri, 1943–1952.
             Kamil Sham'un, 1952–1958.
             Fuad Shihab, 1958–1964.
             Charles Helou, 1964–   .

Masqat and Uman

Traditional sultanate with close treaty ties to Great Britain since 1839.

Persian Gulf Federation

Formed in 1968 by Bahrayn, Qatar, and seven Trucial shaykhdoms (among which the oil-rich Abu Dhabi and Dubai). Traditional principalities, protected by the United Kingdom under various nineteenth-century treaties; withdrawal of British military units scheduled for 1971.

Saudi Arabia

Traditionalist monarchy of house of Saud originating in central Arabian region of Najd, enlarged 1913–1926 by successive annexation of al-Hasa, Asir, Hijaz, etc.; name Kingdom of Saudi Arabia adopted 1932.

Amir (later King) Abd al-Aziz ibn Saud, 1897–1953.
King Saud ibn Abd al-Aziz, 1953–1964.
King Faysal ibn Abd al-Aziz, 1964–   (exercised royal powers as Crown Prince,
1958–1960 and 1962–1964).

Southern Yemen

Aden became a British Crown Colony in 1839; 22 tribal areas, most of them with treaty
relations with Britain, were known as the Aden Protectorate. These two were merged, in
1962, as the Federation of South Arabia. Federation overthrown shortly after independence (1967), and Republic of Southern Yemen proclaimed.

Syria

Part of French Mandate, 1920; proclaimed independent republic, 1941; French occupation
withdrawn, 1946; union with Egypt in United Arab Republic proclaimed in 1958 and
dissolved in 1961.
  Shukri al-Quwwatli, President, 1943–1949, 1955–1958.
  Successive coups install military regimes under Colonels Husni Zaim (March, 1949),
    Sami Hinnawi (August, 1949), and Adib Shishakli (December 1949–1954).
  Gamal Abdul Nasser, President of U.A.R., 1958–1961.
  Nazim al-Qudsi, President of Syrian Arab Republic, 1961–1963.
  General Louay al-Atasi, 1963.
  General Amin al-Hafiz, 1963–1966.
  Dr. Nur al-Din al-Atasi, 1966–   .

Turkey

First Republic proclaimed 1923 after collapse of Ottoman Empire and victorious campaign
of nationalist government at Ankara. One-party regime until 1945, transition to
democracy interrupted by military coup of 1960. Second Republic proclaimed in 1961
with democratic-parliamentary governments.
  Presidents: Kemal Atatürk, 1923–1938.
        Ismet Inönü, 1938–1950.
        Celal Bayar, 1950–1960.
        Cemal Gürsel, 1961–1966.
        Cevdet Sunay, 1966–   .
  Prime Ministers: Adnan Menderes, 1950–1960 (Democratic party).
        Ismet Inönü, 1961–1965 (Republican People's party; coalition).
        Suat Hayri Ürgüplü, 1965 (Justice party; coalition).
        Süleyman Demirel, 1965–   (Justice party).

Yemen

Traditional autocracy under Imams of Zaydi Shiah, attained independence upon Ottoman
defeat, 1918. Coup of 1962 leads to proclamation of Yemen Arab Republic and civil war
between Republican and monarchist forces.
  Imam Yahya, 1904–1948 (assassinated).
  Imam Ahmad, 1948–1962.
  Imam al-Mansur billah Muhammad al-Badr, 1962–   .
  President Abd Allah al-Sallal, 1962–1967.
  Abd al-Rahman al-Iryani, Chairman of the Presidential Council, 1967–   .

Political Systems in Flux

                    The countries in this group are the ones
which, more than any others, have given the Middle East its reputation for
political instability. Political change in these systems has been frequent and often

violent; their recent history is replete with riots, *coups d'état,* assassinations, and revolutions. One basic problem which contributes to this state of flux has already been touched upon—the prevalent desire of the politically active groups to create strong and powerful nation-states in the face of inherited handicaps, including a history of foreign political and economic interference and domination and, in the case of the Arab countries, conflicting loyalties to the separate existing states and to the ideal of a unified Arab nation. The other chief unstabilizing factor has been the conflict between the conservative, oligarchic interests represented by royal dynasties and large landowners, on the one hand, and the rising Westernized urban groups, on the other. But the precise mixture of external and internal unstabilizing forces differs from country to country.

Egypt

Egypt became an Arabic-speaking country as a result of the seventh-century conquests of the early Caliphs (or temporal successors of Muhammad). Like Syria and Iraq, it was conquered by the Ottoman-Turkish sultans in the sixteenth century. Yet Egypt, of all the Arab and all the Middle Eastern countries has the most distinct geographic identity. The Nile is the common bond of the inhabitants, and vast stretches of desert mark the country off from its neighbors. In the late Middle Ages, Egypt was ruled by the Mamluks, a caste of warriors and landowners originally imported as slaves from the Turkish tribes of the Caucasus. Even under Ottoman rule the Mamluks enjoyed a great deal of autonomy, enhanced by the steady decline of central power in Istanbul.

The Napoleonic invasion (1798–1801) marks the beginning of modern Egyptian history. Muhammad Ali, who established himself as ruler shortly after the departure of the French, was a shrewd and energetic autocrat. A soldier of Albanian origin he had little education himself but keenly appreciated the value of education for his subordinates. He also had a rare grasp of the importance of economics as a basis of military and political power. Muhammad Ali was the first Middle Eastern monarch to send young men to Europe for their studies. He improved irrigation and introduced the planting of cotton, which has since become the mainstay of the Egyptian economy. In various military campaigns Muhammad Ali's forces first came to the aid of his nominal overlord the Sultan and at length turned against him. If it had not been for the threat of European intervention in 1840, Muhammad Ali might have taken over the rest of the Ottoman Empire.

The speculative boom of the 1860s and the following slump left the Egyptian government with a huge foreign debt and forced the Khedive to turn the collection of revenues over to a Debt Administration representing British and French financial interests (see above, chap. 2). An abortive military coup under Urabi Pasha, aimed at establishing some form of constitutional checks over the monarchy, led to renewed European intervention and at last to occupation by the British. For nearly a quarter century an able British banker, Sir Evelyn Baring (later Lord Cromer), as Consul General in Cairo, was the country's undisputed ruler, and Cromer's successors continued his work of improving irrigation, streamlining administration, and augmenting revenue.

But politically, the British occupation remained vulnerable. Since it was initially conceived as a temporary intervention on behalf of creditor interests, neither the British nor the Egyptians ever settled down for a long quiet symbiosis. There was much intellectual and political ferment toward the turn of the century, expressed in the religious reform movement known as Islamic Modernism and led by Muhammad Abduh, and in the National party of Mustafa Kamil. Economically, too, it was under Cromer's administration that the race between economic growth and population first gained momentum: cotton production doubled by 1914, but so did population.

Since Egypt remained nominally part of the Ottoman Empire, which in 1914 joined the German side in the First World War, the British feared (wrongly as it turned out) widespread enemy sympathy. They therefore declared Egypt a protectorate but sweetened the pill with a promise of postwar independence. Independence therefore became the goal of vocal elements in the educated middle class and it received increasing support from the urban masses. The demonstrations that welcomed a self-appointed Egyptian delegation (Wafd) on its return from the Paris Peace Conference gave the country its first taste of mass politics. The British decision to exile the Wafd's leader Sa'd Zaghlul only enhanced his popularity and heightened the pitch of agitation. In a precedent for what became a classic pattern, Zaghlul was brought back as prime minister. Still, negotiations remained deadlocked and the declaration of Egypt's independence of 1922 has the dubious distinction of being the only such document issued by the imperial power over the protests of the leaders of the supposedly independent country.

The interwar period was marked by an intermittent three-way wrangle between British, royal palace (supported by various oligarchic politicians), and the Wafd. An overall reconciliation took place in 1936. The British agreed to relinquish their control over defense and foreign policy in times of peace. In return the Wafd government of Mustafa Nahhas, under the impact of Italian expansionism, agreed to allow British peacetime occupation of the Suez Canal and wartime operations throughout the country. Yet once again the outbreak of war exacerbated relations. British tanks surrounding the royal palace in 1942 forced the ouster of a mildly pro-Axis government to restore the Anglophile Nahhas. His renewed cooperation with the British and widespread corruption in his party, however, undermined Nahhas' position, and the temper of postwar politics grew more and more fiercely anti-British. As in the 1920s, British reaction to Egyptian claims to the Sudan further exacerbated feelings, and defeat in the Palestine War of 1948 added to the prevailing bitterness. The religious-radical Muslim Brotherhood organized a guerrilla campaign in the Suez Canal zone and elsewhere, and there was a wave of political assassinations.

A military coup on July 23, 1952, overthrew King Faruq and the corrupt parliamentary regime. After an initial seesaw contest with General Naguib, Colonel Gamal Abdul Nasser by 1954 managed to suppress not only the traditional parties but also the Communists and the Muslim Brethren. The main supports of his regime have been the army, the local administration centralized under the ministry of the interior, an efficient secret police, and organized labor. Above all, his early successes in domestic and foreign policy gave Nasser a genuine popularity on which he was able to draw again and again in times of later adversity. The ambitious Aswan Dam project, financed with Russian help after 1955, provided a visible impetus to economic development—even though population increases continued to devour the surplus. But the foreign successes were even more striking: British agreement to evacuate the Suez Canal (1954), Russian agreement to supply arms (1955), Nasser's ability to counter Western pressure by nationalization of the canal (1956), the rapid withdrawal of British, French, and Israeli troops after the invasion of 1956, the union with Syria (1958). By design, by exploitation of rivalries between the major powers, and by sheer luck, Nasser had established himself as the embodiment of the hopes of Arab nationalism far beyond the borders of Egypt. Internally, the sequestration of foreign business, nationalization of banking, and some redistribution of landed estates undermined the traditional position of minorities and the post-Mamluk oligarchy. Even though the dissolution of the union with Syria, the defeat in Yemen in the early sixties, and the debacle of the third Arab-Israeli war (1967) greatly tarnished Nasser's image, he managed to quell unrest in the armed forces and among students with apparent ease. Whatever the setbacks, the mere fact that Nasser had remained in control for a decade and a half marked a unique achievement among recent rulers in Arab "systems in flux."

Syria

Syria, for most of its history, has been a geographical concept rather than the designation of a well-defined state with unchanging borders. In the early sixteenth century, it was incorporated by conquest into the Ottoman Empire, along with the neighboring Arab regions of Iraq and Egypt. Until the First World War, Syria was usually thought to include Lebanon, Palestine, and Transjordan—that is, the western half of the Arab Fertile Crescent. It was in the cities of this Syrian region—Damascus, Beirut, Jerusalem—that the first intellectual stirrings of Arab nationalism came to be felt within the decaying Ottoman Empire. Only with the advent of the so-called Young Turks—i.e., the Union and Progress movement—to power within the empire (1908–18) did dissatisfaction with Ottoman rule lead to conspiratorial political organization, chiefly among students, army officers, and other urban intellectuals.

The first moves toward anti-Ottoman revolt came early in the First World War when the Syrian movement made contact with the entourage of Sharif Husayn, the Ottoman-appointed guardian of the Holy Cities of Mecca and Madinah in the Hijaz. The connection was cemented when the Sharif's second son Faysal was initiated into one of the Syrian conspiratorial societies known as al-Ahd (or The Covenant). Stern repressive measures by the Ottoman authorities, such as the summary hanging of several dozen Syrian Arab leaders including a member of the Ottoman senate, and severe food shortages during the war, served to spread and consolidate the nascent revolt. When, in 1916, Sharif Husayn disavowed his loyalty to the Ottoman Empire and, with the encouragement and support of British agents and advisers such as T. E. Lawrence, began to move northward at the head of a body of Arab troops, many of the Arab officers who managed to desert the Ottoman ranks joined him, and the progress of the Arab revolt was watched with anxious anticipation in Syria. Toward the end of the war, Faysal and Lawrence made their triumphal entry into Damascus.

The political future of Syria remained in suspense for two years after the war. Faysal spent much of his time in Paris to plead personally the cause of

Syrian independence before the peace conference. An American commission of inquiry under Henry C. King and Charles Crane, dispatched at President Wilson's insistence, found that politically articulate Syrians overwhelmingly favored independence, although if some tutelage were required they decidedly preferred this to be under American or British rather than French auspices. But in early 1920, Britain honored its secret wartime agreements by assigning Syria (including Lebanon but not Palestine and Transjordan) to a French mandate under the newly formed League of Nations. Meanwhile, an assembly of Arab notables at Damascus, known as the Syrian National Congress, proclaimed Faysal king of Syria. But soon French troops, even before the expiration of a perfunctory ultimatum, surrounded the hills of Damascus and after a brief shelling of the city ejected Faysal.

French policy under the mandate throughout the interwar period was clearly predicated on the age-old imperial principle of divide and rule. The predominantly Christian district of Lebanon was enlarged to include the port cities of Beirut, Sayda (Sidon), and Tarablus al-Sha'm (Tripoli) and a sufficient portion of the hinterland to create a new entity (known initially as "Greater Lebanon") which included a bare Christian majority along with Sunnis, Shiis, and Druzes. The Druze-populated mountains to the south of Damascus were given their separate administration, and so was the northern Syrian coast with its Alawi population, named État des Alaouites. But the precise administrative divisions of French mandate into from two to five separate units varied frequently. In the end, two units, Syria and Lebanon, emerged.

French rule had been established by military force, and although it was welcomed by many of the Christian elements in Lebanon, it was deeply resented by most Syrians. A rebellion originating in the Druze mountains in 1925 quickly spread to the rest of Syria, and was suppressed with some difficulty. In 1928, the French at length convened a Syrian constituent assembly, and a first parliamentary constitution went into operation under the French mandate in 1930. Attainment of independence was delayed by French-Syrian disagreements over the future of the district (or sandjak) of Alexandrette. This Syrian region on the Turkish border had been accorded a special status in a French-Turkish agreement of 1921, and now that Syrian independence became a real prospect, the Turks claimed autonomy for this area with its mixed Arab-Turkish population. Over loud Syrian protests, the sandjak was given autonomy in 1938 and the next year decided to join Turkey (having changed its name to Hatay in the meantime—meaning, in line with Atatürk's Hittite-Sumerian mythology, "Hittite country").

Franco-Syrian relations still were in a protracted deadlock when the Second World War broke out. At first, the country was under control of the Vichy government, but in 1941 Free French and British troops took over in Syria, accompanying their occupation by a solemn promise of postwar independence (the so-called de Gaulle-Lyttleton agreement). The French withdrew their last troops early in 1946—after having been bluntly reminded by the British of their wartime agreement.

Syrian political leaders, who had rallied in a single "National Bloc" during most of the French occupation, soon were embroiled in bitter quarrels. One group advocated alignment with Iraq and Jordan in inter-Arab politics, another argued for alignment with Egypt and Saudi Arabia. The first group tended to favor merger or federation within a Greater Syria (including Lebanon, Transjordan and, it was hoped, Palestine) or within a Fertile Crescent scheme, whereas the second insisted on independence and maintenance of republican institutions against the dynastic aspirations of the rulers of Iraq and Transjordan. The Arab defeat in the Palestine War greatly aggravated the political situation. Student demonstrations and riots became endemic, and the stage was set for a succession of military coups—no less than three of them occurring in 1949. The leader of the last of these, Colonel Adib Shishakli, managed to retain power for five years and to restore a measure of order under a stern dictatorship. His overthrow in 1954 led to a resumption of parliamentary intrigues, punctuated by army revolts, riots, demonstrations, and assassinations.

The Syrian political scene from 1954 to 1958 presented the general spectacle of a sharpening of alignments. Syria had long been jealous of its hard-won independence and, in the late forties and early fifties, was the only Arab country which roundly refused American foreign aid. In the mid-1950s, Nasser's demands for Arab unity found a strong resonance among Syrian leaders, who had always been Pan-Arab by conviction and sentiment but had viewed with profound suspicion the schemes propounded by the conservative, British-allied monarchs of Jordan and Iraq. By 1956, Syria, like Egypt, leaned heavily toward the Soviet bloc and received generous shipments of Communist arms. On the domestic political scene, the merger of two radical political groups in the Arab Socialist Renaissance (Ba'th) party under Akram Hawrani created a strong agitational force. At the same time, Syria was the only Middle Eastern country where a Communist party operated legally, and Khalid Bakdash, the party's chief, was triumphantly returned to parliament. In 1958, the internal struggle for power among several rival military factions, the Ba'th, and the Communists came to a head. At length, the Ba'th and one of the anti-Communist military groups resolved upon a merger of Syria with Egypt—hoping thereby to thwart an imminent Communist take-over and confident that Nasser with his great popularity and international prestige would be able to check Communist influence in the future.

In this manner, the United Arab Republic—the first concrete if partial accomplishment of hopes for Arab unity—was born. For a while, it appeared as if this first measure might set off a snowball effect. Distant Yemen joined the United Arab Republic in a loose and vaguely conceived confederation labeled the United Arab States. Muslim leaders in neighboring Lebanon fought a pitched battle against the corrupt oligarchic regime of Christian president Kamil Sham'un. King Husayn of Jordan and his conservative ministers were facing a mounting tide of popular unrest. The July, 1958, revolution in Iraq drowned the narrow oligarchic regime of that country in a savage bloodbath. And the changeover in Saudi Arabia from spendthrift King Saud to his brother Faysal brought to power in the richest Arab country a prince sympathetic to Nasser's Pan-Arab aspirations. Soon, however, the intervention of American marines in Lebanon and of British troops in Jordan slowed down the momentum of change. General Qasim in Iraq asserted his authority in several tense encounters against the Communists, on the one hand, and against military insurgents in league with Nasser's U.A.R., on the other. The "United Arab States" remained a diplomatic fiction. Thus, by the end of 1958, the initial impetus toward Arab unity under Nasser's leadership appeared to have stalled.

Within the United Arab Republic, too, unity was more easily proclaimed than implemented. The administration of Syria by Egyptian military and civilian officials was increasingly resented by Syrians. Although Syria has a large agricultural development potential, especially in its portion of Mesopotamia, overpopulated, foreign-exchange-starved Egypt could make no dramatic contribution to it. Several years after the proclamation of the U.A.R., moreover, the legal and economic systems of Egypt and Syria still remained separate. When, in the summer of 1961, Nasser's government attempted to proceed with the long delayed administrative and economic integration, the result was the secession of Syria from the three-year-old union, brought about by a revolt of the Syrian military carried out so smoothly and swiftly that Nasser was forced to accept the result with whatever show of amiable grace he could muster. Quick recognition of Syria's reestablished independence by the major powers indicated the success of the most immediate aim of the 1961 coup. But the elections held toward the end of the year showed alignments as inconclusive as those of 1945–49 and 1954–58. Soon Syria relapsed into a pattern of intense political intrigue among various ideological factions, including moderate and radical Ba'this and Communists, each with its own allies in the armed forces. Once again military coups rather than constitutional or electoral processes became the normal means of change from one government to the next.

Lebanon

Lebanon, like Syria, attained formal independence in 1943 and actual independence with the departure of French troops in 1945 and 1946. The internal politics of the country continued to be based on a fundamental agreement worked out among the leaders of the various denominations during mandate days. Under this formula, the president of the Republic was to be a Maronite Christian, the prime minister a Sunni Muslim, and posts in the cabinet and other parts of the government were to be filled by Christians and Muslims in a ratio of six to five. The commercial preoccupations of a country consisting largely of the biggest Arab port and its truck-farming hinterland served to cement this *status quo*. The Arab boycott of Israel since the Palestine War of 1948 brought considerable economic advantages to Lebanon. Commercial airlines in their globe-circling runs made Beirut rather than Tel Aviv their major Middle Eastern stop, and Western firms installed their branch offices in Beirut. The huge flow of oil revenues into Arab countries, especially after the "fifty-fifty" profit-sharing agreements of the early 1950s, brought huge deposits to the banks of Lebanon, whose policy of free trade provided a sharp contrast to the currency restrictions and tariffs of neighboring states. During the summers, the resort towns on the breezy slopes of Mount Lebanon attracted affluent tourists from sweltering Egypt, Iraq, and Saudi Arabia. And the inflow of foreign money set off a gigantic building boom in the business and residential sections of Beirut.

The careful denominational arithmetic of the governmental system nevertheless concealed growing dissatisfaction. The "six to five" formula was based on the last population census taken as far back as 1932. There was much evidence that in the intervening decades the higher birthrates of the Sunni and Shii populations and the greater propensity among the Christians to emigrate to the Americas had converted the slight Christian majority of 1932 into a Muslim majority by mid-century. Yet the vested interests of the delicately equipoised political system prevented the taking of any new census.

In the meantime, Nasser's popularity rose high among the Muslims, the pro-Western policy of Christian politicians aroused much resentment among those with neutralist or Pan-Arab leanings, and the increasing corruption of the administration led to periodic outbursts, activist groups among the Maronite Christians and the Sunni Muslims usually being the chief protagonists. In 1952, President Bisharah al-Khuri was ousted in a bloodless coup. By 1958, the opponents of his corrupt and ineffective successor, Kamil Sham'un, were arming themselves, and for several months the country's economy and public life were paralyzed by a sporadic civil war. The government thereupon called upon the assistance of American military forces, which was granted under the so-called Eisenhower Doctrine. The brief intervention of American marines in the summer of 1958, and the conciliatory policy of Sham'un's successor, Fuad Shihab (who resigned as commander in chief in order to assume the presidency), restored the country to its previous normality and profitable commercial pursuits.

The aftermath of the Arab-Israeli war of 1967 brought renewed crisis. Although the government of the country did its best to stay out of the conflict, the Palestinian refugees in its borders knew no such restraint. By 1969, the government forces had all but yielded control over the southeastern corner of the country to the Palestinians directed by the militant al-Fatah and supplied with Russian arms from Syria. Conversely, Israeli retaliation raids periodically hit Lebanon.

Jordan

The country of Jordan has the distinction of having the most artificial boundaries, the poorest endowment in natural resources, and the least-developed feeling of civic loyalty of any country in the Middle East. Although government publicity handouts grandiloquently purport to trace the country's history to the Nabataeans toward the beginning of the Christian era, the creation of the state of Transjordan (as it originally was called) was the result of the peace settlement imposed on the Arab parts of the Ottoman Empire after the First World War. In the British-French agreement of 1920, the parts of geographic Syria north of Lake Huleh and the Druze mountains were assigned to the French mandate of Syria and Lebanon; those to the south to a British mandate of Palestine. The boundaries of this original Palestine mandate were drawn in such a way as to connect, albeit through stretches of desert, with the other British mandate of Iraq.

In 1920, Abd Allah, second son of Sharif Husayn, led a group of Bedouin warriors from the Hijaz toward the Syrian border, presumably to avenge the earlier ouster of his brother Faysal as king of Syria. The British dissuaded Abd Allah from this adventure, and in return installed him as amir (ruler) of the parts of the Palestinian mandate to the east of the River Jordan and the Dead Sea. This decision not only was designed to create a local principality loyal to

Britain, but also to exempt the inland desert portion of Palestine from the provisions of the Balfour Declaration (on which see below in the section on Israel). Abd Allah's tribal forces were transformed, under the command of a British officer, Brigadier John Bagot Glubb (Glubb Pasha), into a tightly knit, well-disciplined force known as the Arab Legion.

Transjordan now had a ruler, an army, and a capital (the small town of Amman, once founded by Circassian refugees from the Caucusus who were resettled by mid-nineteenth-century Ottoman sultans)—but it lacked most other tangible assets. Its desert dunes were unsuited for agriculture, and no minerals were discovered under them. Its coastal city of Aqabah, on the northeastern end of the Red Sea, was undeveloped as a port and its possession, moreover, disputed by neighboring Saudi Arabia. All imports, therefore, had to come via the Palestinian ports of Haifa or Tel Aviv (and since 1948 via Beirut and Damascus). After the Second World War, Transjordan was released from mandate status and given the official appellation of Hashimite Kingdom of Transjordan (Hashim being the tribe of the Prophet, from whom Sharif Husayn claimed lineal descent). The country, however, continued to be administered in close cooperation with British advisers, and its annual deficits to be covered from the United Kingdom treasury.

In the Palestine War of 1948, Abd Allah's Arab Legion made the best showing among the Arab states against the military forces of nascent Israel. When the war ended in a draw, the Transjordanian forces were in possession of most of the Arab-populated parts of Palestine, including Old Jerusalem and the Judaean hill country to the north and south. In 1949, Abd Allah annexed these eastern parts of Palestine on the opposite side of the Jordan to his country, whose name appropriately was shortened to Hashimite Kingdom of Jordan. This *fait accompli* was deeply resented by other Arab countries, who briefly thought of expelling Jordan from the Arab League. It also led to Abd Allah's assassination in 1951 by followers of the mufti of Jerusalem, Hajj Amin al-Husayni, whose hopes of ruling an Arab Palestinian state Abd Allah had thwarted.

The incorporation of the rump of Arab Palestine nearly tripled the kingdom's population; one-third now consisted of the original Transjordanian Bedouin tribes, one-third of the resident Palestinian population, and one-third of Arab refugees from parts of Palestine included in the State of Israel. The Palestinians, with their far higher level of education and economic advancement chafed at the conservative rule of the King, his Bedouin shaykhs, and their British advisers. The refugees, crowded into miserable camps, were resentful of any government which did not secure the extinction of the Israeli enemy and their resettlement in their former homes. With the influx of refugees and other Palestinians, Ammam rapidly was transformed from a small desert outpost into a bustling metropolis of a quarter of a million people.

Abd Allah's son Tallal was declared insane shortly after his succession, and his infant son Husayn succeeded to the throne, at first under the regency of the Queen Mother. By 1955, Nasser's propaganda denouncing all remnants of British hegemony as perfidious imperialism and urging unification of all Arab countries was beginning to make a profound impression in Jordan. In a short but convulsive *coup d'état*, Jordanian officers of the Arab Legion forced the ouster of Glubb Pasha and other British officers and advisers. Young King

Husayn fought with desperate courage for the preservation of his throne, tacking now with and now against the winds of revolutionary nationalism. The original British subsidy was replaced by a combination of British and American financial support, and those British advisers who remained were now less conspicuously displayed. The merger of Syria and Egypt early in 1958 was countered by the announcement of an Arab Federation between Jordan and Iraq, but the bloody revolution in Baghdad in July 1958 exploded that short-lived and ill-defined legal scheme. As United States marines landed in Lebanon, King Husayn retained his throne by virtue of the brief return of British troops, whose departure he had earlier been forced to demand.

The Arab-Israeli war of 1967 resulted in an even graver threat to the survival of Husayn's monarchy and of the country itself. Husayn was the only Arab leader who personally led his troops in battle, and his army acquitted itself better than that of Egypt. Yet it was Jordan that suffered most in the aftermath of the war—having lost the populous and relatively prosperous west bank and been forced to receive a new flood of destitute refugees. Once again the King was forced to rely on the loyalty of his Bedouin army, and he found it hard to control the bands of Palestinian guerrillas operating from his territory, let alone to ward off periodic Israeli retaliation raids.

Just as the country had suffered most from the consequences of the war, it stood to gain most from peace with Israel, which might bring the return of much of the lost western territory and perhaps an outlet across Israeli territory to the Mediterranean. By the fall of 1968, there accordingly were reports of intense if informal diplomatic explorations between Jordan and Israel. Yet any final agreement would constitute a decisive break by Jordan with her Arab allies (for whom intransigence was less expensive) and lend renewed strength to all the the internal forces of unrest. Even in the absence of new peace overtures, King Husayn found it difficult to prevent armed clashes between the guerrillas and his regular army which assumed an increasingly defensive position.

Iraq

Iraq combines a variety of enviable economic assets with a traditional structure of society which only recently has entered a phase of revolutionary modernization. Unlike Syria and Jordan, it has sizable petroleum resources (especially around Mosul in the north and Kirkuk in the northeast). In contrast to oil-rich Saudi Arabia and Kuwayt, it also possesses arable land and, in the huge Euphrates and Tigris rivers which traverse it from north to south, abundant water to irrigate it. Yet, despite its memories of high civilization in the days of Sumer, Babylon, Assur, and down to the Baghdad caliphate of Harun al-Rashid, Iraq became one of the culturally most stagnant areas of the Ottoman Empire. Not until the late 1950s, for example, were the first efforts made to transform a number of junior colleges in Baghdad into a modern university. Along with Iran, Iraq is therefore not just a poor but a truly "economically underdeveloped" country, where abundant assets such as topsoil, water, and petroleum income wait to be transformed through skillful management and labor into the basis for a thriving industrial and agricultural economy. Together with Lebanon, Iraq also is the most heterogeneous Arab country of the Middle East, its population being slightly over one-half Shii Arab, about 30 per cent Sunni Arab, and about 20 per cent Sunni Kurdish.

British troops from India landed in the Persian Gulf during the First World War, and by 1917 had occupied much of Iraq, extending their control to the oil-rich Mosul area in the days following the Ottoman armistice of 1918. The establishment of a postwar mandate regime under British aegis was complicated by a bitter and widespread revolt of the Shii tribes of the Middle Euphrates region. By 1921, the British, observing the outward appearances of a plebiscite, managed to install Sharif Faysal (recently ousted as king of Syria) as king of Iraq, a move that suggested itself both because of the former close cooperation between the Sharif and his British advisers and because most of the Arab officers who had rallied to Faysal were of Iraqi origin.

Under Faysal I, Iraq developed into a smoothly functioning, tight political oligarchy. The central core of the ruling circle was formed by the army officers around Faysal, most prominent of whom was General Nuri al-Said, long-time chief of staff and more than a dozen times prime minister of the country. From the beginning of the mandate period, this group of officers of middle-class background was joined by members of old Baghdad families, such as the Gaylanis and Pachachis, and some Basrah and Mosul notables, such as the Umaris and Bash-Ayans. The inclusion of several minority representatives helped to establish a modicum of political unity amid the prevailing religious and ethnic diversity. Thus Sasun Hasqayl, a Jewish banker from Baghdad, frequently held the finance portfolio, and one or another member of the Baban family—descended from a long line of Kurdish chiefs in Sulaymaniyyah but long since urbanized and Arabicized—was a necessary complement to almost every cabinet. The leaders of the Shii tribes and various Shii *mujtahids* were regularly given parliamentary seats and later also admitted to the cabinet. The challenge of incipient party movements with a strong rhetorical appeal to the intelligentsia and the urban masses was diverted in the late 1940s by the promotion of some of their leaders to an occasional cabinet portfolio.[1]

Although Iraq's formal constitution was that of a constitutional monarchy with a cabinet responsible to an elected parliament, the true lines of authority were neatly reversed. Thus not a single one of the forty-odd cabinets which governed in rapid succession between 1920 and 1958 was ousted by a parliamentary vote of nonconfidence. Most of them fell through disputes among the ministers or through intrigues by dissatisfied members of the oligarchy intent on speeding their own rise to cabinet office. Once a new cabinet was installed, it was customarily allowed to dissolve parliament, and a seasoned minister of the interior could, by judicious promises of political rewards and threats of punishment, produce a pliable majority. A large proportion of members of parliament, especially from the tribal areas, were regularly returned without opposition. Behind this oligarchic parliamentary façade, British interests—represented by advisers in all government ministries and the royal palace, by British garrisons at the Habbaniyyah airport and elsewhere, and by the Iraq Petroleum Company (owned jointly by British, French, Dutch, and American interests but admin-

[1] This paragraph is adapted from Almond and Coleman, *Politics of the Developing Areas,* pp. 434ff.

istered by British managers)— played a prominent and well-entrenched role.

By a treaty in 1930, Iraq became the first of the League of Nations mandates to be given its formal independence, to take effect with it admission to the League in 1932. But several fissures soon began to appear in the delicately balanced structure. The death, in 1933, of King Faysal I, who combined the skills of a traditional desert leader with those of a modern diplomat, deprived the oligarchic system of its natural point of reference. (Faysal's son Ghazi was a racing-car addict who drove to his death in 1936; for many years thereafter, the royal office was administered by Prince Abd al-Ilah as regent for the infant King Faysal II.) In 1936, a group of army officers seized power in a bloody coup, promising to pursue a more vigorous nationalist policy. Bakr Sidqi, the military leader of the new regime, had earlier won his spurs in a large-scale massacre of the small Assyrian-Christian minority, who had become well-hated in mandate days as favorite recruits in the British-organized Iraqi military levies. Some other military coups that followed proved to be rather mild and ritualistic affairs—a few planes zooming over Baghdad, a declaration of disloyalty from some army units stationed near the royal palace—and the startled citizenry might hear from the morning news bulletin that yet another military-civilian junta had taken over the government.

A final coup, in the spring of 1941, came close to starting a revolution which would have destroyed the earlier basis of British and oligarchic rule. The leader of the 1941 coup was Rashid Ali al-Gaylani, a dissident member of a distant branch of the Baghdad patrician clan. He sought support in his violent anti-British and Pan-Arab policy by appealing for military assistance to the Vichy French forces in Syria and to the Nazi Germans, who just then were finishing their *blitzkrieg* occupation of Greece and Crete several hundred miles further west. In Baghdad, in the meantime, regent Abd al-Ilah narrowly escaped with his life while crouching on the floor of the American ambassador's car. In Habbaniyyah, a small British garrison desperately fought off vastly superior Iraqi forces. But Rashid Ali's urgent appeals for outside help went largely unheeded. Turkey refused to allow the transit over her railways of any German military equipment destined for Syria or Iraq. Above all, Hitler had no conception of the strategic value of the Middle East and instead viewed his Balkan conquests only as a preparatory maneuver for his long-cherished Russian campaign. After a few tense days, Glubb Pasha's Arab Legion raced across the desert to relieve the beleaguered Habbaniyyah garrison, Rashid Ali escaped to Saudi Arabia, and the previous condominium of the royal house, the British, and the local oligarchy was restored.

After the Second World War, the Pan-Arab, anti-British, anti-Zionist, and vaguely socialist slogans of radical intellectuals found an increasing echo in the press and among the urban masses, yet by and large conservative, pro-Western forces retained the upper hand. As early as 1942, Nuri al-Said had propounded his Fertile Crescent unification scheme, a plan that enjoyed the tacit encouragement of the British government, which had been greatly frightened by its narrow escape from strategic calamity during the Rashid Ali revolt. After the war, however, Egypt's scheme for a more comprehensive if loosely structured Arab League won out over any federation plans. In 1949, street demonstrations in Baghdad forced the resignation of Iraq's first Shii premier, Salih Jabr, who had returned from

Britain with a treaty that would have prolonged British rights to Iraqi bases, even though on terms far more favorable to Iraq than existing arrangements. In 1950 and 1952, Iraq revised its concession agreement with the Iraq Petroleum Company to bring royalties up to the "fifty-fifty" level, thus benefiting from the hard fight waged by Musaddiq in Iran without having to duplicate its violence or tension.

In 1954 and 1955, Iraq, once again under Nuri al-Said's leadership, concluded a military alliance with Turkey, Iran, Pakistan, and Britain known as the Baghdad Pact and corresponding to the "Northern Tier" concept of Middle Eastern defense assiduously expounded by United States Secretary of State John Foster Dulles. Although the conclusion of that pact, and Iraq's accession to it, was widely hailed in the Western press as a political gain, it was significant that this (largely illusory) military gain was achieved at the cost of closer Egyptian and Syrian alignment with Russia, and of heavy-handed suppression of all potential opposition within Iraq. Several months before the conclusion of the pact, Premier Nuri prohibited all Iraqi political parties and closed down all newspapers except for a handful specially licensed by the government. The spectacular Egyptian deal for arms deliveries from Czechoslovakia and Russia in September 1955 was a direct response to Iraq's pro-Western move, and the "anti-imperialist" propaganda emanating from Cairo and Damascus found a hearty resonance among the muzzled critics of Nuri's policy.

The revolution which broke out in Baghdad in July 1958—by far the bloodiest and cruelest the Middle East had yet experienced—brought much of the delicately balanced diplomatic, political, and social structure of the last decades crashing down with a loud report. Key figures of the *ancien régime,* including King Faysal II, Crown-Prince Abd al-Ilah, and General Nuri al-Said were killed, and their bodies savagely mutilated or dragged through the streets. Surviving leaders of the monarchic period were held for trial in televised, demagogical star-chamber proceedings. The military leaders of the revolution, headed by General Abd al-Karim Qasim, denounced Iraq's membership in the Baghdad Pact and adopted a neutralist foreign-policy course eagerly backed by the Soviet Union.

Iraq since 1958 has followed a political pattern not unlike that of Syria. Political factions competed in revolutionary rhetoric and socialist pronouncements while engaging in complex and bitter intrigues. Foremost among these competing groups were several factions of the Ba'th party (which in the 1950s spread from Syria to Jordan and Iraq), the Communists, and various military cliques. Traditional rivalries, such as those between Sunnis and Shiis, or between Baghdad, Mosul, and Basra now had to hide behind such ideological façades. Since 1958, even more clearly than after 1936, the military have remained the ultimate arbiter in politics. A palace coup in 1963 replaced Qasim with Colonel Abd al-Salam Arif. Upon the latter's assassination, the government came to be headed by his brother, Abd al-Rahman Arif, who in turn was overthrown by a coup in 1968, contrived by a moderate Ba'thi faction.

Despite the revolutionary and anticapitalist rhetoric of these successive régimes, and despite their periodic flirtations with Russia, from which Iraq was receiving military and economic aid, the operations of the Western-owned Iraq Petroleum Company continued. The third Arab-Israeli war of 1967, unlike the second war of 1956, did not even occasion any prolonged stoppage of the flow of oil to the West. Although Iraq by the late 1960s thus could count on nearly $400 million in hard-currency petroleum revenues, and although land, water, and population provide some of the other necessary ingredients, there has been little progress in economic development—whether in agriculture, industry, or education and manpower training.

An intermittent rebellion among the Kurds in the northern mountains, led by their tribal leader Mustafa Barzani, was a major source of difficulty for each successive government in Baghdad. The government's policy usually would alternate between conciliation and military repression—the first running into the Kurds' deep-seated distrust, and the second into the natural barriers of the mountain terrain which favored the indigenous population.

Saudi Arabia

Saudi Arabia may be listed among the Middle Eastern "political systems in flux," although it still retains many features of a more traditional political structure. The present state has its origins in the tribal dynasty of Saud which in the eighteenth century established itself in the central Arabian region of Najd in close cooperation with the Wahhabis, a puritanic Islamic sect. At the beginning of the nineteenth century, a Wahhabi uprising throughout the Arab peninsula was crushed with some difficulty by the forces of Muhammad Ali of Egypt on behalf of the Ottoman Empire. By the end of the century, however, Najd had come under the control of the house of Ibn al-Rashid of the rival Shammar tribal confederation. Ibn Saud (or with his full name, Abd al-Aziz ibn Abd al-Rahman Al Faysal Al Saud), the most illustrious member of his house, grew up in exile at the court of the shaykh of Kuwayt. With the decline of Ottoman power during the First World War, Ibn Saud managed to reconquer his ancestral domains from the Ottoman vassals of Shammar. In 1926, his troops defeated Sharif Husayn and annexed the Hijaz (i.e., the Red Sea coastal region around the Holy Cities of Mecca and Madinah). By the 1930s, Ibn Saud had established full control over the peninsula with the exception of Yemen and of the British-protected areas along the coast from Aden to Kuwayt, and the Saudi Bedouin warriors, recruited into a militant religious brotherhood, were imposing the austere Wahhabi version of Islam upon the conquered populations. The revenues of the newly consolidated kingdom at this time mostly consisted of pilgrims' fees and of tribute levied from various tribal vassals.

The discovery of oil deposits in the Persian Gulf coastal region of al-Hasa before the Second World War, and the beginning of large-scale production at war's end by the American-owned Arabian-American Oil Company (Aramco), soon began to revolutionize the country's financial and social structure and to enhance its international position. The pilgrims' dues were reduced and at length abolished, and subordinate tribal leaders now were subsidized from the royal treasury, as were the members of the sprawling royal house and their Cadillac-riding retinue. A year before Ibn Saud's death in 1953, a new "fifty-fifty" profit-sharing agreement with Aramco brought close to a quarter-billion dollars annually of oil revenues into the royal treasury. Ibn Saud's decadent son and successor Saud ibn Abd al-Aziz soon managed to overspend even these lavish sums and had to rely increasingly on advances from Aramco. From 1958 to 1960, and again in 1962, Saud's royal powers were transferred to his brother Crown Prince Faysal, and in 1964 Saud was persuaded to abdicate in Faysal's favor. The new monarch was a skilled and economical administrator—and coincidentally the annual amount of oil revenues during his reign rose sharply to around $1 billion. The growing petroleum industry, with its related construction, refining, and transport enterprises, was employing an increasing number of Arabs from the more advanced countries such as Palestine and Syria. Many of these looked with distaste on traditional monarchy, whether in its camel or its Cadillac version, and instead expected national salvation from the dynamic leadership of Egypt's Gamal Abdul Nasser.

Yet by the 1960s (especially with Syria's secession from the United Arab Republic in 1961 and the failure of the renewed unity negotiations between Egypt, Syria, and Iraq) Nasser's star began to wane. And the first clear confrontation between Nasser and the Saudis took the form not of subversion within the kingdom but of a war by proxy outside. Since the republican regime proclaimed in Yemen in 1962 soon obtained military aid from Egypt, King Faysal in his turn supported the royalist side with money and arms. Although this Saudi support never enabled the royalists to win a clear military victory, the withdrawal of Nasser's decimated troops by 1967 amounted to a clear defeat for any Egyptian ambitions to turn a republican Yemen into a springboard for a take-over of the Arabian peninsula. After the defeat in the Arab-Israeli war of 1967, the Saudi-Egyptian rapprochement had proceeded far enough to make it possible for King Faysal, along with the rulers of Kuwayt and Libya, to compensate Nasser for the loss of $200 million annually in Suez Canal revenues. By the late 1960s, the future of monarchy in Saudi Arabia seemed more secure than it had been in a decade or more.

Iran

Despite its distinct Shii and Persian national heritage, Iran displays most of the features of the neighboring Arab-Sunni "political systems in flux." The 1905 revolution imposed a scheme of representative constitutional government on the spendthrift Shahs of the Qajar dynasty, but partition of the country into British and Russian spheres of influence (1907) and a royalist countercoup of Muhammad Ali Shah (1908) thwarted the efforts of the rising middle-class reformers. During the First World War, Ottoman, German, British, and Russian troops freely operated in neutral Iran. After the war, Bolshevik forces, pursuing White Russian contingents across the Caspian, installed a secessionist Soviet-style government in the northern province of Gilan. In 1919, a treaty that would have transformed Iran into a British protectorate was signed by bribed cabinet ministers but never ratified by the national parliament (or *majlis*).

Two years later, Riza Khan, a sergeant who had risen to command of the Czarist-trained Cossack Brigade and distinguished himself by ousting the Gilan Soviet regime, seized power in Tehran. In 1925, Riza deposed the Qajar dynasty and had himself proclaimed shah with the newly adopted family name of Pahlavi. For sixteen years, Riza Shah ruled the country with a heavy, despotic hand, building railroads and hospitals and otherwise trying to modernize the country, and establishing a modicum of central control over the tribal areas in the south. In 1941, Britain and Russia decided to occupy Iran in order to open a Western supply line to the Russian front. Since the pro-Axis Riza Shah proved uncooperative, he was sent into exile to South Africa (where he died in 1944), and replaced with his son Muhammad Riza. The occupation was normalized in a tripartite treaty, in which the two allies undertook to evacuate their troops six months after the end of hostilities.

It was in Iran that the cold war between Russia and the West began even before the end of the hot war against Germany and Japan. The Russians diverted most of the grain from the fertile northwestern province of Azarbayjan for their own use, while Communist-inspired newspapers blamed the resulting food shortages in southern Iran on capitalist exploitation by the British occupants. In 1944, the Russians pressed for a large-scale concession for oil exploration throughout northern Iran, a move which prompted the *majlis,* led by an aristocratic lawyer named Muhammad Musaddiq, to pass a law forbidding any cabinet member to even enter negotiations for a foreign concession without explicit parliamentary approval. In 1945, a separatist Communist regime under the name of Azarbayjan People's Republic was set up in the shadow of Soviet bayonets, some of the leading personnel consisting of party members who had won their spurs in Gilan in 1919 and weathered the intervening years in Muscovite exile.

After the war, freedom of the press and of political agitation was restored, and a large number of ephemeral political parties sprang up. Representation in the *majlis,* however, continued to be weighted heavily in favor of large landowners and other established members of the ruling oligarchy. Weak governments were formed in rapid succession by shifting coalitions among their oligarchic cliques. In the large cities, agitation by nationalist orators and street demonstrations inspired by the Communist Tudah party or by the religious-fundamentalist followers of Mullah Kashani resulted in riots, assassinations, and political turmoil. But a series of daring maneuvers by Premier Ahmad Qawam (1946–47), ably supported by Western diplomatic moves in and out of the United Nations Security Council, succeeded in removing the Communist stranglehold on Iran. The Soviets, faced with the choice of holding on to their position in Azarbayjan or to play for a share in the government of the country as a whole, withdrew their troops in return for three Tudah seats in Qawam's cabinet and a promise of favorable consideration for their old concession demand. After the restoration of central authority in Azarbayjan, the concession proposal was roundly voted down in a *majlis* controlled by Qawam's followers, and the threat of a march on Tehran by the powerful Qashqai tribe prompted the ouster of the Tudah ministers.

A major new crisis erupted when negotiations between the Iranian government and the British-owned Anglo-Iranian Oil Company for a larger Iranian share of royalties broke down. A new government under Musaddiq in 1951 unilaterally nationalized the company's assets. Musaddiq's policy of Iranian national self-assertion and of strict honesty within the traditionally corrupt central government won strong support from the rising urban middle classes who flocked to his National Front party. Yet Musaddiq was unable to maintain oil production after the departure of British staffs and in view of the boycott on oil transport imposed by the international companies. Internally, Musaddiq's reform measures antagonized the traditional oligarchy and prompted an increasingly dictatorial course that brought him in conflict with the Shah, the army, and even his erstwhile supporters among the religious followers of Kashani. By 1953, Musaddiq seemed in full controll, and the Shah fled to Rome for fear of his life. But a dramatic armed coup, led by General Fazlullah Zahidi, ousted Musaddiq overnight and restored Shah Muhammad Riza to power.

The Shah's restoration brought a reversion to the oligarchic clique politics of the pre-Musaddiq era. A 1954 agreement, mediated by United States negotiators under Averell Harriman, settled the oil conflict. While petroleum properties remained nationalized, most of their operation was entrusted to an international consortium, in which the former Anglo-Iranian Oil Company (now rebaptized British Petroleum Company) held a minority interest, other shares being controlled by the leading international (American, Anglo-Dutch, and French) companies with Middle Eastern oil interests. Royalties were divided according to the "fifty-fifty" formula earlier agreed upon in Iraq and Saudi Arabia. Although most of the oil income and ample American foreign aid funds were set aside for a major scheme of agricultural and industrial development, most of the monies, amid the prevailing governmental corruption, seeped into private hands.

In contrast to Musaddiq's neutralist foreign policy, the new regime joined the pro-Western Baghdad Pact in 1955. Within the government, the Shah and his palace advisers retained effective power; yet the Shah's widely publicized acts of land donations did more to entertain the readers of the illustrated press than to relieve the prevailing sharecropping system by which the cultivators retained a mere fifth of their produce. By the late 1950s, two political parties, playing at government and opposition, were officially licensed, but the rigging of two successive elections in 1960 and 1961 caused widespread dissatisfaction. Student demonstrations in the late spring of 1961 forced the appointment of a reform administration under Premier Amini. But discontent smoldered on. In Moscow, Premier Khrushchev announced the overthrow of the Shah as an official aim of Russian policy. Successive royal cabinets bravely promised drastic reforms while followers of the outlawed National Front and other discontented elements were waiting for new revolutionary opportunities.

Yet by the mid-1960s, Iran was embarked on a series of social, economic, and political changes that were at last cutting below the surface. The key factors in this "white revolution" were the enormous increase in oil revenues, the determination of government planners to invest these oil monies in economic growth, and a land reform program that was beginning to produce a real change in the status of the peasantry. The revised land reform law was designed less for theoretical perfection than for ready application, and it revolutionized the age-old system whereby absentee owners had controlled the lands of many villages, the villagers working as sharecroppers usually for one- or two-fifths of the crop. Under the new system, landowners were allowed to retain one village of their choice and would be compensated for all others on the basis of the taxes they had been paying (thus ensuring a low rate of compensation without any need for an expensive and disputatious cadastral survey). Peasants were allowed to work their old plots as owners, on condition that they joined with others in an agricultural cooperative and paid for the land in small annual installments at low interest.

Far-reaching as were these changes in agriculture, the major effort of economic development went into transport, industry, and education. Although the oil boom and wholesale migration to the cities tended to widen the gap between rich and poor, especially in the cities, the peasantry, for the first time perhaps in Persian history, began to develop a sense of self-reliance. And although discontent among the college-educated class did not disappear overnight, a growing proportion of the young intellectuals began to find employment in the various economic offices of the government or in private enterprise and through such employment to obtain a stake in the system. All in all, it was far less apparent in the sixties than it had been in the fifties that reliance on the armed forces remained the mainstay of the Shah's rule.

Similarly, although friendly relations with the United States continued, the Shah managed to effect a remarkable rapprochement with Khrushchev's successors, culminating in an agreement whereby Russia is to supply a steel mill and other forms of economic aid in return for natural gas (previously burnt off as waste) that is to be sent by pipe to the Soviet Union.

Other States

The coastal areas of the Arabian peninsula from Kuwayt to Aden were firmly under British control or influence by the end of the First World War. A generation later, the progressive withdrawal of Britain from its imperial commitments around the Indian Ocean led to a series of realignments. These international changes, in the case of many of the Persian Gulf states, came at a time of rapid expansion of petroleum production (in Kuwayt since the 1950s, in Abu Dhabi, Dubai, and other Trucial states mainly since the late 1960s). In one way or another, most of these Arabian costal states therefore may also be said to be political systems "in flux."

Kuwayt became fully independent of Britain in 1961, and because of his huge oil income the shaykh of Kuwayt soon became an important power in inter-Arab politics. The booming oil industry has brought a large influx of Arabs from socially more advanced countries such as Palestine and Lebanon, and nationalist sentiments among these run high. The shaykh's willingness since the 1967 war to pay an annual subsidy to the Arab countries bordering on Israel and to Arab Palestinian guerrillas clearly was a move intended to placate such nationalist opposition.

The island of Bahrayn, technically an independent principality, is one of the oldest oil producers of the Middle East, and one of the few areas of the region where the limit of available resources has been reached, so that production is slowly declining. Iran from time to time puts forward a territorial claim to Bahrayn. But the island is all the way across the gulf near the Saudi shore, and Saudi opposition to the Iranian claim would seem to be the best guarantee of Bahrayn's independence.

In 1968, Bahrayn joined with Qatar and seven so-called Trucial shaykhdoms to the east in a Persian Gulf Federation. Jealousies among the various rulers and Saudi and Iranian competing interests delayed such an arrangement, but in view of the final British withdrawal, announced for 1971, common interest in the maintenance of hereditary thrones prevailed. The discovery of large quantities of petroleum in Abu Dhabi and Dubai were beginning to revolutionize the economy of the Trucial coast, and there were tentative plans to build a giant airport and harbor.

The sultanate of Masqat and Uman is larger than all the others states just mentioned, but its oil production is relatively modest and there are few other economic assets. The hereditary ruler, always nominally independent, relied on British advice and protection as long as these were available.

Even more barren and inhospitable to human habitation is the area of Southern Yemen, whose only asset is the port of Aden with its enormous refinery and fueling facilities. The territory was once known as the Aden Crown Colony and Protectorate, but British withdrawal and proclamation of independence in 1967 were followed quickly by the overthrow of the (now unprotected) petty sultans and the formation of a People's Republic. The basis of the new state was military support and socialist rhetoric, much as in the republican parts of neighboring Yemen or in more distant Syria and Iraq.

Modern Political Systems

Whereas the Middle East's "systems in flux" display an unstable mixture of modern and traditional features along a more or less continuous scale, the two political systems which may properly be classed as "modern" each represent a case *sui generis*. Israel's population consists mainly of immigrants, the earlier ones mostly from Europe. Their political and cultural background has little in common with that of the traditional Middle East. And the very process of immigration and adjustment to a newly founded society and commonwealth has given its population an adaptability that contrasts sharply with the traditionalism of much of the remaining population of the area—an adaptability which the older, European immigrants have also managed to convey to the more recent and more numerous Jewish immigrants from southwest Asia and northern Africa. In many of its more specific political and social features, Israel resembles more nearly one of the smaller multiparty democracies of Europe than it does its immediate Asian neighbors.

Turkey must be included in the category of "modern political systems" with somewhat greater hesitation, for its evolution has been gradual and differs from that of the Arab countries and of Iran more in degree than in kind. Yet, on balance, the modern features are the predominant and more dynamic ones, although events of the late 1950s and early 1960s have shown that modernization does not always proceed smoothly or without temporary turbulence.

Israel

The State of Israel, proclaimed on May 15, 1948, has its roots in Zionism, the movement originating among European Jews toward the turn of the century aimed at combating the effects of European anti-Semitism by creating a Jewish nation-state. Although the movement's founder, the Viennese Theodor Herzl, briefly thought of locating that state in Uganda, the bulk of the Eastern European followers of the movement had no question that the only location for such a state could be Palestine. The Balfour Declaration of 1917, in which the wartime British Foreign Secretary announced Britain's support for "the establishment in Palestine of a national home for the Jewish people," for the first time propelled Zionism to the stage of great-power diplomacy; and with the installation of the postwar British mandate over Palestine, the goal of Zionism seemed within reach.

Both the Balfour Declaration and earlier Zionist pronouncements had made passing reference to the preservation of the rights of non-Jewish populations in Palestine, as if Palestine were a country with a primarily Jewish population interspersed with miscellaneous ethnic minorities. In fact, however, the 1920 population of Palestine consisted entirely of Arabs (96 per cent, to be precise), and the right which the Palestinian Arabs most cherished was the preservation for their country of that Arab character which it had had for close to thirteen centuries. An early decision of the mandate administrators to give Arabs and Jews each their separate institutions of community self-government served to sharpen the contrast between the two groups, and the stimulation to the Palestine economy (brought by large-scale Jewish immigration supported with outside funds) only enhanced the Arabs' nationalist consciousness. Like their neighbors in Egypt and Syria, the Palestine Arabs soon learned that demonstrations, obstruction, and ultimately direct and violent action were most likely to impress their demands upon the imperial power.

Very soon after the beginning of the mandate regime, the British, in various ways, began to circumscribe their support of Zionist aims. But each such step—from the separation of Transjordan from Palestine proper in 1921 to the imposition of annual immigration quotas in the White Paper of 1939—was likely to increase rather than attenuate Arab demands. The White Paper, coming at a time when Hitler's extermination campaign made the need for a haven for Jewish refugees more desperate than it had ever been, altogether exacerbated relations between the mandatory and the Jewish population. While the official paramilitary arm of the Jewish community, the Haganah, replied to Arab terrorist attacks with restraint and supported the British defense effort during the Second World War, more radical Jewish organizations such as the Irgun Zvai Leumi and the Stern Gang hit indiscriminately at Arab and British targets.

By 1945, the situation in Palestine had deteriorated into a fierce, three-cornered civil war. Neither the British government nor an Anglo-American cabinet commission (1946) nor the United Nations General Assembly (1947) was able to devise a solution that would have been acceptable to both Arabs and Jews—most proposals being roundly rejected by both. The partition scheme advanced by the United Nations, moreover, would have divided the country into a checkerboard of disconnected strips of Arab and Jewish territory, a solution which could have worked only on the basis of that very intergroup harmony whose absence made partition imperative. At length, the British declared their mandate terminated as of May 14, 1948, giving ample notice so that Jewish leaders were able to prepare the proclamation of Israel for the following day, with the veteran Zionists Chaim Weizmann and David Ben-Gurion as president and prime minister.

Even before that proclamation, the neighboring Arab states (Egypt, Syria, Transjordan, and later Iraq) had begun to move their troops across the Palestinian borders. In the war that ensued, the Arabs—vastly superior in number but overconfident, and vague and uncoordinated both in their military strategy and in their political aims—proved no match for the well-disciplined and determined Israeli forces. When an armistice was negotiated with United Nations mediation in early 1949, Israel was in control of eight-tenths of the former mandate territory, including the newer parts of Jerusalem, the fertile coastal plain, the Galilaean hills in the north and the Negev desert in the south. Nearly a million Arab refugees at war's end were crowded into miserable camps either in the eastern parts of Palestine annexed by Jordan or in the Egyptian-occupied diminutive and crowded Gaza Strip.

With the existence of the new state assured through military victory, immigration was thrown open to all Jews who wished to come to Palestine. This included, at first, numerous refugees from Europe and, in addition, almost the entire Jewish populations of Iraq, Yemen, Iran, and other Middle Eastern states where community relations had sharply deteriorated as a result of the Palestine War. All in all, the population of Israel more than doubled in the first decade after independence. From the beginning of Jewish settlement in the mandate days, Hebrew had been revived as the official language of the community, and the strong social pressure of an immigrant society made this linguistic conversion effective, particularly among the second generation. Only for the remaining Palestinian Arabs was Arabic retained as an official second language.

Ample funds, collected by supporters of Zionism outside Israel, particularly the annual United Jewish Appeal in the United States, financed the settlement of these immigrants, as well as a far-flung program of agricultural and industrial development sponsored by the government and by a number of autonomous semi-public agencies. Other payments, such as reparations received from West Germany in the late 1950s, contributed to the development program. Thanks to these economic efforts and outside support, Israel's standard of living from the start was substantially above that of its Middle Eastern neighbors; yet by the early 1960s, Israel could cover only about half her annual imports from current exports.

The continuing hostility of the neighboring Arab states not only necessitated large defense expenditures but also aggravated the foreign-payments situation. Initial hopes for a more permanent peace settlement to follow upon the armistice agreements of 1949 were quickly dissipated, and even efforts to work out some kind of technical agreements, such as on division of the waters of the Jordan River among Syria, Lebanon, Jordan, and Israel, faltered against the Arab's refusal to recognize the very existence of the new state. Throughout the early 1950s, moreover, border incidents and retaliation raids, especially along the Jordan frontier and the Gaza Strip, multiplied. The economic boycott instituted by the Arab League forced Israel to import petroleum from Iran or from as far away as Venezuela, whereas the Iraq Petroleum Company's pipeline from Kirkuk to Haifa lay dry.

At the same time, Israel's export industry was deprived of most of its natural markets and instead had to seek outlets in more distant Asian and African countries. The Arabs' measures of economic warfare, on the other hand, were plainly insufficient to inflict any decisive damage on Israel's economy or on her political chances of survival. On the contrary, the Israeli-British-French attack on Egypt in 1956 once again demonstrated Israeli military strength even against an opponent recently armed with large amounts of Soviet equipment. Partly under the impact of this second military encounter and partly as a result of United Nations garrisoning of the Gaza Strip, Arab border attacks and Israeli retaliation raids all but ceased.

The interlude of relative peace ended abruptly in the late spring of 1967 as President Nasser of the United Arab Republic asked for the departure of United Nations forces from Gaza and Sharm al-Shaykh, replaced them with Egyptian military units, and announced his intention of cutting off Israeli shipping through the Strait of Tiran. Israel predictably interpreted these moves as preparations for war and, as in 1956, resolved to strike first. Within hours after the opening of the war on June 5, 1967, the Israeli airforce had destroyed most of its Egyptian counterpart, and in six days Israeli troops stood along the Suez Canal, the entire length of the River Jordan, and the crest of the Golan heights in Syria.

The situation resulting from the June war was fraught with explosive tensions. The Arab defeat was even more calamitous than in 1956—it involved three countries, it was inflicted by Israel alone, and the Israelis seemed to be prepared for a long stay. The Egyptian airforce was quickly rebuilt with rapid Russian deliveries, and Arab Palestinians stepped up their sabotage activities within the occupied territories and Israel proper. Yet sabotage alone was no substitute for reconquest; the Egyptians remembered from bitter experience that mere arms without adequate training and organization would not ensure victory, could indeed lead to new defeats. Jordan, deprived of nearly half of its population, found itself unable to control the guerrilla bands operating from its territory, and one wrong move on the slippery diplomatic or internal political scene might cost King Husayn his throne or his life. Similarly, Lebanon saw itself forced to give over its southeastern district, along the Syrian and Israeli borders, to the Palestinian guerrillas as a base of attack—and to Israeli counterraids by bombers, artillery, and occasional armored forays.

Israel had tripled the territory under her control, shortened her military lines, and, through control of Sinai, gained enough additional air warning time so as to relieve her of any need for a first-strike strategy in a future conflict. Israeli leaders—supported by public opinion—appeared determined not to surrender such gains except in the unlikely event that Arab governments, by sitting down with Israel in direct negotiations, should publicly disavow their desire to "push Israel into the sea." Meanwhile, the addition of nearly one million Arabs to the area under Israel's control compounded her problem of internal security. It also presented Israeli leaders with a long-run dilemma: whether to dilute the Jewish character of their state by according full civic rights to those Arabs, or whether to dilute the egalitarian character of their society by denying them those rights.

The dreary pattern of infiltration and sabotage by Arab Palestinian commandos and of Israeli military retaliation intensified during the winter of 1968–69. The arms race was continuing, suggesting the possibility that the Soviet Union and the United States as the chief suppliers would be increasingly drawn into the conflict. Outside efforts at settlement showed little promise. The Security Council resolution of November 1967 blandly juxtaposed the Arab demand for withdrawal from occupied territories and the Israeli demand for recognition and a signed peace. Although a United Nations emissary, Ambassador Gunnar Jarring, shuttled patiently from one Middle Eastern capital to another for about a year, his mission only appeared to confirm that neither side was willing to make the first move regarding these two demands. The Israelis, moreover, insisted on direct negotiations, something the Arabs flatly refused. Negotiations among the major powers—the United States, the Soviet Union, Great Britain, and France —were begun mainly at Russian and French insistence. Yet the United States and the Soviet Union remained far apart in their views; nor was it clear how a Big-Two or Big-Four solution, assuming it could secure the assent of the powers, could be made palatable to the countries of the region. By 1970 there was little prospect of settlement whether by direct negotiation or through unsolicited big-power mediation. Instead, the earlier pattern of infiltration and retaliation had escalated into almost daily air battles over Egypt and less frequent raids and counterraids along the Lebanese, Jordanian, and Syrian fronts.

Turkey

The Republic of Turkey originated in the War of Independence (1919–23), in which the Anatolian rump of the Ottoman Empire successfully fought for the preservation of its sovereignty in the face of Greek invasion and Allied partition plans. The new state's most significant political asset has been the presence of dedicated political leaders who were able to continue a tradition of responsible service dating back to Ottoman days. Where the Arab successor states of the Fertile Crescent had to build up their administrative staffs from minute beginnings, Turkey could draw on a manpower pool that had served an empire three or four times its size. Once the Turkish ruling class found itself relieved of the incubus of this decaying empire, it concentrated with renewed vigor on the far more manageable task of building up a small but viable nation-state.

Not only was there continuity in personnel, there also was a gradual transition in political institutions. The War of Independence was fought, ostensibly in the name of the captive Sultan in Allied-occupied Istanbul, by the bulk of the demobilized Ottoman army with the support of numerous civilian "Societies for the Defense of Rights" and under the leadership of Turkey's outstanding military figure of the World War I period, Mustafa Kemal (later known as Atatürk). The Kemalists' foreign-policy plank, known as the "National Pact," was formulated in the summer of 1919, two years before their *de facto* government at Ankara got around to drafting a provisional constitution; their Grand National Assembly had been directing the affairs of the country for two and a half years when, after the final victory in 1922, it declared that the sultanate had ceased to exist as of 1920, and the Republic was not officially proclaimed until October 29, 1923, following upon the international recognition of Turkey's hard-won sovereignty in the peace treaty of Lausanne. At every turn, foreign realities took precedence over the exigencies of the domestic scene.

Mustafa Kemal had insisted during the War of Independence that all questions of internal reform be resolutely postponed and had based his appeal on a combination of nationalist and religious-traditional motifs. Now, with the foundations of the new state firmly laid and political leadership concentrated in his Republican People's party, he proceeded with a rapid program of secularist legal and cultural reforms. The caliphate and the Ministry of Religious Affairs were abolished in 1924 and schools unified under a secular Ministry of Education; in 1925, the dervish orders were closed and dress modernized by government decree; in 1926, European civil and criminal codes replaced the traditional Islamic law; and in 1928, Latin letters were substituted for the Arabic script. The 1930s brought an intensive program of public industrial development, known as *étatisme,* concentrating on railroads, textiles, and steel production. The annexation of the Hatay, completed in 1939 shortly after Atatürk's death, realized a hope he had long personally cherished.

During the presidency of Atatürk's successor and close collaborator, Ismet Inönü (1938–50), Turkey managed to steer a careful course of neutrality amid the belligerent camps, declaring war on Germany and Japan in 1945 *pro forma,* just in time to be invited as a founding member of the United Nations. The economic dislocations of wartime mobilization contributed to the rapid postwar growth of opposition parties, notably the Democratic party which took power in a major landslide victory in Turkey's first free and honest election in 1950. Large-scale American economic and military assistance, extended under the Truman Doctrine and subsequent programs, led to a second major wave of industrial and agricultural development. By her support of United Nations action in Korea (1950), her admission to the North Atlantic Treaty Organization (1952), and her leadership in concluding the Baghdad Treaty (1954, relabeled the Central Treaty Organization in 1958), Turkey became firmly committed to the West in the face of the continuing threat of Russian expansion toward the Middle East.

Turkey's political development since 1945 provided the first occasion when a firmly rooted dictatorial one-party regime yielded to a system of open party competition voluntarily and in an orderly manner. The peasant majority, long the neglected entity in Turkish as in other Middle Eastern politics, was beginning to play an increasingly active and self-assertive role, and in the cities, newspapers, political rallies, and party organization multiplied. The democratic experiment also implied a number of gradual but fundamental changes in political course. The policy of *étatisme* was abandoned in favor of encouragement of private enterprise, at least in manufacturing industries. Agricultural development through the building of roads, irrigation dams, grain elevators, and extensive farm mechanization corrected the earlier one-sided emphasis on industry, and a number of restorative reforms (such as the introduction of religious schooling and the reversion to the Arabic prayer call) played up to the peasantry's conservative, antisecularist bias. But the peasants' unconcern with the niceties of liberal constitutionalism also made possible a gradual and systematic erosion of the very political freedoms that had permitted the ascent of the peasantry's champion, the Democratic party.

Just before their second landslide victory in 1954, the Democrats under Premier Adnan Menderes confiscated the assets of Inönü's Republican People's party and closed down the smaller Nation party. By increasingly repressive measures, the press, the universities, and the courts were deprived of their political independence. As a prolonged and severe economic crisis resulted from Menderes's overambitious economic development program, all critical voices were silenced and opponents of the increasingly corrupt ruling clique subjected to violent harassment. In the spring of 1960, the authoritarian regime of Premier Menderes and President Bayar was ousted in an almost bloodless coup resulting from student demonstrations in Istanbul and Ankara and from the resolute intervention of the army, which refused to let itself be used as a tool of repression of mounting popular discontent.

The military junta, under the presidency of General Gürsel, was soon split into a moderate wing dedicated to restoration of democracy and into a radical one eager to proceed to some vaguely defined authoritarian experiment of social and political regeneration. The majority sided with the moderate position, ousted the radicals, called a constituent assembly which drafted a new checks-and-balances constitution in record time, but approved the death sentences imposed on Menderes and two of his associates.

The first four years of the Second Republic (1961–65) were a transition period. A number of coalition governments under Inönü of the People's party ruled with precarious and shifting support in the bicameral parliament. Gürsel was elected to a full presidential term and his colleagues on the junta given life senatorships; in return the military command protected the nascent regime against a number of attempted coups by frustrated radicals within the officer corps. The former followers of Menderes's Democratic party, split into three rival groups in 1961, had rallied around the Justice party by 1965. The advent of Süleyman Demirel's Justice party government in 1965 signaled a step toward renewed political stability and toward reconciliation between the leaders of the peasant majority on the one hand, and the military-bureaucratic establishment on the other.

The Cyprus conflict of 1963–64 provided the occasion for a reassessment of Turkey's foreign policy. American pressure to keep Turkey from using the right of military intervention on behalf of her conationals on the island caused profound resentment, coming as it did after a long period of close military and economic cooperation—or, as some saw it, Turkish dependence on the United States. The Kremlin's shift from a pro-Greek to a more pro-Turkish attitude in the Cyprus conflict therefore encouraged a limited rapprochement between Turkey and the Soviet Union, although Turkey remained a loyal member of NATO and retained her close economic ties with the West.

Traditional Political Systems

Yemen and Afghanistan are the only remaining traditional political systems of the Middle East. Both countries, by virtue of their inaccessible location, escaped the imperial impact of the modern West, Afghanistan in particular being aided by its buffer situation between British India and Imperial Russia. Both countries were being increasingly drawn into the orbit of international politics after the Second World War, and it is safe to assume that their internal political structure will gradually be modified, moving increasingly in the direction of the Middle Eastern "systems in flux."

Yemen

Yemen occupies the extreme southern mountainous and fertile part of the Arabian peninsula. For centuries, it was at least nominally a dependency of the Ottoman Empire, but since the beginning of the twentieth century, Ottoman troops were engaged in a protracted losing fight to assert the authority of the distant central government. After the First World War, Yemen became independent under its local ruler, elected by the *ulama* of the Zaydi branch of the Shiah in San'a, who claims the title of Imam by virtue of his direct descent from the Prophet. The Imam's absolutism was limited in theory by the sovereignty of Qur'anic law, but in practice more effectively by the poverty of communications in his primitive country and by the everpresent threat of palace revolt and assassination.

Imam Ahmad, in such a palace revolt, succeeded the aged Imam Yahya in 1948; by 1960, he himself had been the victim of three assassination attempts in a single year, and the princes of the royal house who had not earlier become victims of the Imam's retaliation were preparing to dispute the succession. Yemen's nominal confederation with the United Arab Republic in 1958 (under the title United Arab States) had little practical political impact but gave new impetus to the Imam's longstanding border claims against the neighboring British colony and protectorate of Aden. By the late 1950's, Russian, Communist Chinese, and United States missions were vying in such projects as road building, port development in the Red Sea coastal town of Hudaydah, and mineral exploration throughout the country.

In September, 1962, following Ahmad's death, his successor, Imam Muhammad al-Badr, was deposed by an armed conspiracy under Colonel Abd Allah al-Salal, who proclaimed a Yemen Arab Republic. By the end of the year, Salal's republican forces, with firm support from Egyptian troops, were in control of most of the country, while the deposed Imam was trying to mobilize the peripheral tribes and support from the Kingdoms of Jordan and Saudi Arabia for his declining cause. Yemen's move toward the "systems in flux" had come more rapidly than many observers had expected. A set of protracted negotiations between Egypt and Saudi Arabia beginning in 1965 called for a withdrawal of Egyptian troops and a cessation of Saudi support for royalists. The civil war spluttered on, however, at a lower level of violence with the Republicans in control of the populous areas and the royalists controlling the tribal districts.

Afghanistan

The landlocked mountain kingdom of Afghanistan underwent some of the same crises of threat of foreign occupation and of a seesaw struggle between forces of tradition and reform that beset Turkey and Iran—except that the country's isolation delayed the impact of these modernizing factors until the twentieth century. Afghanistan began as the youngest of the Middle East's traditional states. Its ruling dynasty goes back to a nomadic clan which in the late eighteenth century unified most of what is today Afghanistan and parts of West

Pakistan. But civil wars and rebellions soon again threatened the newly won unity, and the present boundaries did not become stabilized until the late nineteenth century. A major factor in this consolidation was the desire of the British imperial administration in India to maintain Afghanistan as a buffer state between India and Russia. King Amanullah, coming to power by *coup d'état,* was the first ruler to shake off this British tutelage; but his administrative and political reforms, modeled on those of Kemal Atatürk in Turkey and Riza Shah in Iran, ran into strong opposition from the clergy, and Amanullah himself was assassinated in 1929. After some period of confusion, a distant relative, Zahir Shah, was proclaimed ruler, and for over three decades the highest posts in the administration remained in the hands of the king's uncles, brothers, and cousins.

Afghanistan became newly involved with the external world in the 1950s, this time as a result of the arrival of competing American and Soviet foreign aid missions. After some experimentation, Zahir Shah decided to ally himself with the reformist elements in the growing bureaucracy. The royal relatives were replaced by members of this aspiring new middle class, and a representative constitution was proclaimed once again in 1964. Judging by the experience of other Middle Eastern countries, however, it will be some decades before these constitutional and legal changes will have any lasting impact on the traditional social structure and on day-to-day politics outside the capital.

Party Systems and Elections

The preceding survey of dynamic factors in the various political systems of the Middle East makes possible a comparative examination of such essential political features as parties, elections, and organized interests. Throughout this discussion, we shall have to keep in mind the basic distinction between "systems in flux," "modern systems," and "traditional systems." For example, in the traditional countries of Yemen and Afghanistan and in semitraditional Saudi Arabia, no elections have been conducted, no parties formed, and no vocal socioeconomic interest groups organized. Rather, the political process has taken place almost entirely within the royal palace among the members of the ruler's family and among tribal leaders on the periphery. The "systems in flux" and the "modern systems" both have room for parties, elections, and interest groups, yet these perform different functions in each system.

Systems in Flux

In Egypt, Syria, Iraq, Jordan, and Iran, elections have been held in the intervals between dictatorships, but the more decisive forces of change have been the establishment and relinquishment of foreign control and internal *coups d'état* and revolutions. The stakes of the political struggle have generally been not peaceful control of the government within a stable representative system, but change of the regime itself through manipulation and violence. Most parties in these countries have been ephemeral, volatile, and representative of only a small coterie of founders. The nationalist political groupings which formed in Syria and Iraq around the time of the First World War, by the 1920s and 1930s had split into a moderate group inclined toward greater conciliation toward the imperial power and a more radical group pressing for abolition of foreign prerogatives. In Syria, the moderates called themselves the People's party (1924), and the radicals the National Bloc (1928); in the debate on Arab unification and realignment in the 1940s, the Populists sided generally with Jordan and Iraq, the the Nationalists with Egypt and Saudi Arabia. In Iraq, the moderates centered around Nuri al-Said called themselves the Iraqi Covenant in the 1930s and in 1949 the Constitutional Union, whereas the radicals were known successively as the People's party, the National Brotherhood (Ikha, 1931), and the Independence party (1946). A third, rival group was formed in 1951 by the Shii politician Salih Jabr under the name of Socialist Party of the Nation.

One of the most durable party patterns developed in Egypt in the period between the two world wars. The most important group was the Wafd party, originating in the informal delegation (*wafd*) under Sa'd Zaghlul that went to the Paris Peace Conference to press the case for full Egyptian independence. The mass agitation of the following years indicated the overwhelming support for that program among the articulate urban population. If full independence had been attained, the Wafd might well have developed into a broadly based comprehensive-nationalist party not unlike the early Republican People's party in Turkey or the later Neo-Destour in Tunisia. In fact, however, the British were unwilling to surrender control, and the Wafd proved unable or unwilling to force the issue against the opposition of both the King and the British. Throughout the twenties and thirties, the Wafd won overwhelming victories in any reasonably free parliamentary election, but elections would be followed by a new deadlock in negotiations with the British, and the King would then attempt to rule with a set of conservative anti-Wafd ministers. These interludes of royal dictatorship led to the more or less synthetic formation of parties best characterized as "King's Friends"—the Liberal Constitutional party of 1922, the Union party of 1925, and the People's party of 1931 led by Ismail Sidqi. But as the King and his friends ran into overwhelming resistance, they would abandon the attempt, and the cycle would begin anew.

A decade and a half of prolonged deadlock wore out the Wafd. Its support of the Anglo-Egyptian treaty of 1936 compromised its earlier nationalist position. Its willingness to form a pro-British government in 1942, after British tanks had forced King Faruq to oust his pro-Axis ministers, further undermined its popularity. The result was the splitting off of two more radical groups, the so-called Sa'dist Wafd (so named in honor of the founder of the original Wafd) in 1938, and the Wafdist Bloc in 1942. The postwar period saw an increasingly acrimonious contest, at the polls and in parliament, among these three groups— Wafd, Sa'dists, and Bloc. The Wafd in particular was seeking to recapture its nationalist popularity by rejecting proposals for a Western-sponsored Middle East Defense Organization and instead pressing Egyptian claims to the Sudan— occupied by Britain since 1899 under the transparent disguise of an Anglo-Egyptian condominium. A more violent form of political agitation, including assassination of prominent opponents and guerrilla activity in the British-occupied Suez Canal zone, was launched by the Muslim Brethren, who combined a religious-fundamentalist doctrine with highly modern methods of cell organization, social services to members, and mass propaganda. Whereas the Wafd's support came from an efficient countrywide patronage organization, including headmen and small landowners in the villages and place-seekers and government contractors in the capital, the Muslim Brethren based their support mainly on the disaffected urban lower and lower-middle class: artisans, shopkeepers, schoolteachers. The frustration of the defeat of 1948 further exacerbated the Egyptian political climate, and on the eve of the coup of 1952 the atmosphere often verged on civil war.

The Naguib-Nasser dictatorship first asked the parties to purge themselves of corrupt elements but at length closed them altogether. An attempt on Nasser's life in 1954 led to the suppression of the Muslim Brethren who have led a clandestine existence since. The military rulers made several successive attempts to form an official, single party from the top down. The first of these, the Liberation Rally of 1952, has been aptly described as "listless," and the second, the National Union of 1956, as "nebulous." [1] In contrast, the Arab Socialist Union of 1962 has proven more durable and developed greater ideological pretensions. Nonetheless it remains an organization controlled from the center by a regime whose main support derives from the army, the secret police, the bureaucracy, and, to some extent, the trade unions.

In Iran, the demise of Riza Shah's dictatorship in 1941 and the end of the wartime foreign occupation led to an even more bewildering proliferation of parties. These, it has been well observed, generally were "formed from above—a few people grouping themselves around some prominent personality or publishing a newspaper with funds provided by an anonymous capitalist. Their programs were virtually interchangeable and were confined to a series of pious platitudes, of which the 'integrity and independence of Iran' was usually the first. Their names gave even less indication of their policy." [2] Only intermittently would a strong political figure succeed in rallying a more sizable following, such as Zia al-Din Tabatabai's National Will party (1944–46) or Ahmad Qavam's Iran Democrats (1946–47), but these, too, would quickly disband upon the decline of their founder's political fortunes. All these groupings, whether in Iran or in the Fertile Crescent, may be described as "narrowly based pragmatic parties"; [3] they were, in fact, loose factional alignments within a limited oligarchic class. Their sway in parliament and cabinet, moreover, would periodically be interrupted by states of siege or intervals of dictatorship. Thus all parties were dissolved in Iraq from the time of the suppression of the Rashid Ali revolt in 1941 until 1946, and from 1954 until after the 1958 revolution; in Syria from the first of the 1949 coups until the overturn of Shishakli in 1954; and in Iran from the time of Musaddiq's dictatorial rule. (The parties which were officially licensed in 1958 hardly changed this picture, for they had an even narrower base than usual in the support of the royal palace.)

By the 1940s, dissatisfaction with the restrictive oligarchic character of these

[1] Keith Wheelock, *Nasser's New Egypt* (New York: Frederick A. Praeger, Inc., 1960), p. 54.
[2] L. P. Elwell-Sutton, "Political Parties in Iran, 1941–1949," *Middle East Journal*, Vol. 3 (1949), 49.
[3] For an elaboration of this terminology, see Dankwart A. Rustow, "The Near East," in Almond and Coleman, *Politics of the Developing Areas*, pp. 397ff., 408ff.

more traditional parties was giving rise to the formation, among the younger urban intellectuals, of parties with a more militant and more ideological tinge. To the nationalist tenets of the older groups, they generally added a number of socialist demands—for nationalization of banks, redistribution of large estates, and central planning of the state economy. Their political methods ranged from street demonstrations to direct violence. The earliest of these parties originated in Iraq in the early thirties as a socialist study circle known as the Ahali Group. In 1936, it provided the chief civilian support for the first in the long series of Iraqi military coups. From 1946 to 1954, it legally reemerged as the National Democratic party, and in 1958 it was vying with Communists and other groups for civilian popular support under the military regime of General Qasim.

A small agitational and terrorist group known as the Syrian National Social party was founded in Lebanon in 1934 by a Christian emigrant returned from South America, Antun Saadah. Its avowed aim was the merger of Lebanon with Syria, and it has been outlawed in Lebanon since its founder's execution for high treason in 1949, and since 1955 in Syria as a result of its involvement in a major assassination plot. Another S.N.S.P. conspiracy was suppressed in Lebanon in 1962. The most important of these urban radical groups in the Fertile Crescent has been the Arab Socialist Resurrection (Ba'th) party formed in Syria in the 1940s by the merger of two smaller groups under the leadership of Akram Hawrani. The Ba'th party has been the most consistent advocate in Syria of Pan-Arabism, and it has more recently also been active in Jordan and in Iraq. Together with the National Bloc, it was the driving force behind Syria's unification with Egypt in 1958.

The National Front of Muhammad Musaddiq in Iran may be likened to these radical parties of the Fertile Crescent. It originated as one of the small parliamentary coteries which abounded in the *majlis* of the 1940s, but it became a movement with a far-flung organization in the major cities during Musaddiq's dictatorial rule in 1951–53. Although it has been outlawed since that time, it survives clandestinely and, along with the Communist Tudah party, remains one of the latent political alternatives in case the Shah's "white revolution" should fail.

The party picture in Lebanon is complicated by the country's intricate denominational divisions and by the prominence of leading political families. Although candidates may only run for seats assigned to their particular denominations, voters of every religious affiliation can vote for all the denominational seats assigned to their constituencies. The prevailing pattern is therefore one of personal alliances of prominent politicians—such as members of the Edde, al-Sulh, and Bustani families—across religious lines, and parties have been little more than euphonic labels for the resulting alignments. Other groups have a more pronounced denominational base, such as the Phalanges Libanaises (a Maronite group), and the Progressive Socialist party supported by the Druze tribesmen of the south rallied around Kamal Junblat.

Two other political groups have been of considerable importance in the politics of the "systems in flux"—the Communists and various Muslim-fundamentalist groupings. Both are dedicated to radical social change, one toward what it considers the "wave of the future," the other toward what it conceives as the restoration of a purer past. Both have had their strongest appeal among various groups socially displaced by the rapid and uneven pace of urban modernization—communism primarily among the uprooted urban intelligentsia, and Muslim fundamentalism among the urban lower class. Both are inclined toward agitation, street demonstrations, and terrorism. Communism has been illegal throughout most of the Middle East at most times, but there is evidence that the clandestine Communist parties thrive especially well in settings where all party activity is outlawed—including that of their non-Communist competitors—and where their organizational training and tactical and financial support from the Soviet Union can be put to maximum advantage.

Thus the Communist party emerged as a powerful force after the five years of Shishakli's dictatorship in Syria in 1954, and played a major role in the Iraqi revolution of 1958 after a four-year moratorium on political expression. In Iran, the Communists have been operating under the assumed name of Tudah party (party of the masses); it remains to be seen whether the repression of political opinion since the Zahidi coup of 1954 will have benefited them as much as the similar moves of Shishakli in Syria and Nuri al-Said in Iraq. The Major Muslim fundamentalist groups in the Middle East have been the Muslim Brotherhood in Syria, an offshoot of the Egyptian organization of the same name, and the Fidaiyan-i Islam, which carried on a terrorist campaign in Iran in the 1950s. Neither group, however, has matched the strength or prominence that the Muslim Brotherhood attained in Egypt until its dissolution in 1954.

Modern Political Systems

Israel since its inception in 1948 and Turkey from the beginning of the Republic until the 1960 revolution have had representative systems of government based on a one-chamber parliament which elects the president of the Republic and to whom the cabinet is responsible. In Turkey, suffrage was extended to women in 1934; in Israel, all adult citizens, male and female, including immigrants upon arrival, have the right to vote. In both countries, parliament is elected to a four-year term, but may dissolve itself earlier by majority vote. Since Israel has no written constitution, a single vote by a simple majority in the Knesset (parliament) suffices to pass or change any law concerning governmental organization. In the first Turkish Republic, a qualified majority of two-thirds was necessary for the same purpose. Aside from these formal similarities, however, the electoral and party systems of the two countries differ significantly.

ISRAEL. In Israel, voting is according to the list system of proportional representation, with the entire country forming a single election district returning the 120 Knesset members. This extreme form of proportionalism favors a splintering of parties (Table 5-2). On the other hand, the list method of nomination confers considerable power on the party hierarchies, and the parties' close ties to various interest organizations further accentuate the preponderance of their leadership. The country's party system was inherited with little change from the Jewish representative institutions of mandate days and can in part be traced to the factional divisions within European Zionism in the early part of the century.

Although the Knesset has included up to ten major parties, the electorate and

TABLE 5-2

ELECTIONS IN ISRAEL, 1949–1969

Party	Percentage of Vote							Seats in Knesset						
	1949	1951	1955	1959	1961	1965	1969	1949	1951	1955	1959	1961	1965	1969
Communist Parties	3.5	4.0	4.5	2.8	4.1	3.4	4.0	4	5	6	3	5	5	4
Communists	3.5	4.0	4.5	2.8	4.1	1.1	1.2	4	5	6	3	5	2	1
New Communists	—	—	—	—	—	2.3	2.8	—	—	—	—	—	3	3
Socialist Parties	52.1	54.5	52.1	55.0	52.3	51.2	54.0	67	65	64	68	63	67	66
Mapam	14.7	12.5	7.3	7.2	7.6	6.6	—	19	15	9	9	9	8	—
Ahdut Haavodah	—	—	8.2	6.0	6.5	—	—	—	—	10	7	8	—	—
Mapai	37.4	42.0	36.6	41.8	38.2	—	—	48	50	45	52	46	—	—
Mapai (Arab Lists)	—	—	—	—	—	—	3.5	—	—	—	—	—	4	4
United Labor (1965), Alignment (1969)	—	—	—	—	—	36.7	46.2	—	—	—	—	—	45	56
Rafi	—	—	—	—	—	7.9	—	—	—	—	—	—	10	—
State List	—	—	—	—	—	—	3.1	—	—	—	—	—	—	4
Haolem Hazeh	—	—	—	—	—	—	1.2	—	—	—	—	—	—	2
Religious Parties	12.2	11.9	13.8	14.6	15.4	14.0	14.7	16	15	17	18	18	17	18
Mizrahi & Mizrahi Labor (National Religious Party, 1959–)	—	8.3	9.1	9.9	9.8	8.9	9.7	—	10	11	12	12	11	12
United Religious Front	12.2	—	—	—	—	—	—	16	—	—	—	—	—	—
Agudah	—	3.6	4.7	4.7	3.7	3.3	3.2	—	5	6	6	4	4	4
Agudah Labor	—	—	—	—	1.9	1.8	1.8	—	—	—	—	2	2	2
Liberal Parties	20.8	29.6	27.2	24.2	27.3	25.1	26.1	26	35	33	31	34	31	32
Independent Liberals	—	—	—	—	—	3.8	3.2	—	—	—	—	—	5	4
Free Center	—	—	—	—	—	—	1.2	—	—	—	—	—	—	2
Progressives	4.1	3.2	4.4	4.6	—	—	—	5	4	5	6	—	—	—
Liberals (1961), Gahal (1965–)	5.2	19.8	10.2	6.1	13.6	21.3	21.7	7	23	13	8	17	26	26
Herut	11.5	6.6	12.6	13.5	13.7	—	—	14	8	15	17	17	—	—
Others	11.4	—	2.4	3.4	0.7	6.2	1.1	7	—	—	—	—	—	—
Electoral Participation & Total Seats	86.9	75.4	82.8	81.6	81.3	85.9	—	120	120	120	120	120	120	120

its representatives have rather consistently divided into three broad groupings, each with a remarkably stable following. The non-Communist socialist parties have polled from 51 to 55 per cent of the vote, and elected a bare majority of Knesset members (63-68 of the 120). Various religious parties have consistently polled from 12 to 15 per cent of the vote. The third major grouping, including various middle-class free-enterprise and conservative parties, at all elections except that of 1949, attracted around one-fourth (24 to 30 per cent) of the total vote. Among the various splinter groups outside this three-way division, only the Communists have shown any degree of stability, attracting from 2.8 to 4.5 per cent of the voters, mainly from among the Arab minority. It is in each of these three major groupings of socialist, religious, and bourgeois parties that there has been a fair amount of fluctuation, including periodic splits and mergers.

The leading socialist party has been the moderate Mapai, or Israel Labor party, which has never gained a majority of the vote but has always come so close that no combination of other parties has ever been able to form a government without it. In fact it has been Mapai, in coalition with a varying array of smaller parties, which has formed the government ever since independence, which has occupied the most important positions in the government, including the premiership and the ministries of foreign affairs and of defense, and which thus has given multiparty coalition government in Israel a great degree of stability and continuity. Mapai's leadership largely overlaps with that of Histadruth, the all-inclusive Israeli Federation of Labor, which through its affiliates also controls many economic enterprises and plays a prominent role in the country's cultural life. Although Histadruth officially remains aloof from government activities, and in its governing body includes representatives of other socialist and non-socialist parties, it is this strong anchoring in organized labor that has given Mapai its massive support and its durability. Its prominent position in the government itself, of course, has tended to enhance its power. As a successful military figure or an ambitious young man enters into politics, he is likely to find a more prominent career within the "establishment" party than outside it. Mapai's long-time leader was the country's first prime minister, David Ben Gurion. But the fact that Mapai survived a break between the fiery old leader and its organization, headed by the hard-working and able, but colorless, Levi Eshkol, was a clear indication that its fortunes are firmly anchored in organization rather than being subject to the vagaries of personality.

Mapam is the major socialist party to the left of Mapai, and it maintains close ties to the nationwide organization of kibbutzim. Its tone generally has been more militant, its socialist ideology more emphatic than that of Mapai. In the years before Moscow's alliance with the Arabs, it advocated closer relations with the Soviet Union. Although Mapai and Mapam together often commanded a majority of the Knesset, a broad socialist coalition between them has never proved feasible. A third socialist party, Ahdut Haavodah (Unity of Labor), midway in ideological alignment, formed in 1954, entered a common slate with Mapai in 1965, and merged with it in 1968. The 1968 merger also included Rafi, a fourth socialist group. Rafi had originated in 1965 in Ben Gurion's break with Mapai, and as a second colorful leader included Moshe Dayan, field commander of the 1956 and defense minister of the 1967 campaigns. The 1968 merger was warmly advocated by Dayan, who promised to fight for his more activist and unconventional policies within rather than outside Mapai, but it was opposed to the the last by Ben Gurion. In the 1969 election, this broad socialist "Alignment" won 56 of the 120 seats, each of them having been preassigned to the recently merged factions in a complex bargaining process.

There are four distinct religious parties, Mizrahi, Mizrahi Labor, Agudah, and Agudah Labor. All four have an orthodox Jewish following, the two Mizrahi groups representing a more moderate position that fully endorses Zionism, whereas the Agudah groups follow a stricter observance and initially rejected Zionism as a blasphemous attempt by secular leaders to anticipate the Messiah's task of returning his people to the Promised Land. Despite their dedication to doctrinal matters—or perhaps because of it—the religious parties have displayed a great deal of virtuosity at pressure politics and coalition formation. The alignment of parties in the Knesset where they have occupied the precise center of the spectrum, has been such that Mapai has been unable to form governments without them. The price they have exacted has consisted partly in ministerial offices and other patronage and partly in government support for religious as an alternative to secular education and for observance of the religious laws regarding the Sabbath and marriage and inheritance. In the early years, the four religious groups joined in a United Religious Front; in the fifties, the two Mizrahi groups split with their Agudah rivals; and in the sixties there have been three separate slates, the National Religious Front including the two Mizrahi groups, and Agudah and Agudah Labor each running separately.

The smaller Progressive and the larger General Zionist parties have formed the moderate bourgeois opposition to the socialist-religious governing coalition. The General Zionists, in particular, have strong support in the business community. A more extreme right-wing party has been Herut (Freedom), which has its direct roots in the terrorist organizations of the late mandate period, and usually advocated a more activist and expansionist foreign policy. In 1961, Progressives and General Zionists merged, but by 1965 most of the former Progressives split off once again in the Independent Liberal party. At the same time a Herut-Liberal party bloc, known as Gahal, was formed in hopes of challenging the long-time Mapai and socialist hold on the government.

The 1967 occupation of the Sinai Peninsula and the west bank of the Jordan, combined with the refusal of Arab governments to enter direct peace negotiations and with stepped-up Arab guerrilla and terrorist activity, put on the political agenda urgent and explosive questions that cut across many of the conventional political alignments. A broad coalition government, including all parties from Mapam to Herut, was formed, with some of the major debates continuing within the coalition and within the newly formed Labor alignment (Mapai, Mapam, Rafi, Ahdut Haavodah). As time went on, however, the "harder" line of Defense Minister Moshe Dayan and Prime Minister Golda Meir increasingly prevailed over the more conciliatory attitude espoused by the Eshkol government. Besides, an indefinite continuation of the post-1967 occupation of Arab territories seemed the best way of delaying any split in the national coalition over possible peace terms.

TURKEY. The party system of the Turkish Republic, like Israel's, had its antecedents in the political developments of the preceding period. The Defense of Rights Societies which rallied to Mustafa Kemal's call for national resistance in 1919 and 1920 were largely based on the surviving local organizations of the earlier Union and Progress party, although the discredited and fugitive top leadership of the Unionist movement was replaced with new and younger personnel. The nationwide Society for the Defense of Rights of Anatolia and Rumelia, in which these local groups joined in the summer of 1919, fits the model of the "comprehensive-nationalist party," "whose exclusive position results from the rallying of all forces for the attainment or maintenance of independence" in a "power contest . . . primarily between the society as a whole and an actual or potential foreign ruler," and which is "comprehensive in the further sense that it desires not merely a political regeneration but, beyond this, a far-reaching reshaping of society." [4] It thus belongs in the same category as the Indian National Congress and the Tunisian Neo-Destour.

After victory in the War of Independence, Mustafa Kemal in 1923 transformed the Defense of Rights movement into the Republican People's party, which for the next twenty-seven years ruled the destinies of Turkey. An early opposition party, the Progressive Republicians, was formed in 1924 among Kemal's closest military and political associates of the War of Independence days and in protest against his increasingly personal dictatorship. It was dissolved early in 1925 after the party was linked, upon tenuous evidence, with an uprising in the Kurdish provinces. With the suppression of an assassination plot in 1926, with which some of the surviving Union and Progress leaders of the World War I period were associated, the rule of Kemal and his Republican People's party was firmly established without further challenge.

Yet the Kemalist movement differed sharply from the various totalitarian one-party regimes, such as fascism, bolshevism, and national socialism, which were established in various European countries during the same period. It had come to power not in a violent internal revolution but in the external fight against foreign domination. It did not attempt to force a ready-made ideology on a resistant populace; rather its political aims were developed pragmatically step by step, and its six basic tenets (the so-called Six Arrows: Republicanism, Nationalism, Populism, *Étatisme,* Secularism, and *inkilâpçilik,* which is usually translated as "revolutionism" but means, more precisely, fundamental change by legal methods) were codified as late as 1931 after they had already been well embedded in the country's legal system. The benevolent dictatorship of Atatürk and İnönü rather consistently upheld wider political participation as a theoretical ideal to be carried into practice as soon as the level of popular education and other circumstances permitted. The forms of parliamentary cabinet government, moreover, were carefully observed throughout the one-party period, and occasional nay-votes were tolerated without ill consequence for the dissidents.

A brief experiment in 1930 with an officially sanctioned opposition party (the Free party), led at Kemal's behest by his close friend Fethi Okyar, was called off as premature after a mere four months. But in the following years, the Republican People's party (R.P.P.) attempted to broaden its representative base by seating a number of manual workers, women, and members of the non-Muslim minorities in Parliament and by readmitting to the political scene most of the

[4] Almond and Coleman, *Politics of the Developing Areas,* pp. 397, 400.

surviving Unionists and Progressives. In 1939, Ismet Inönü inaugurated another half-hearted experiment of a so-called Independent Group within the parliamentary R.P.P., whose members could hold their separate caucuses and were not to be bound by party discipline. But since the Independents were officially appointed rather than self-nominated, little effective opposition resulted. In 1945, however, with the international pressure of the Second World War relieved, Inönü allowed the formation of opposition parties and, after a hesitant start in the 1946 elections (when gross irregularities in the count distorted the results of a free vote), pledged his administration to evenhanded dealings with government and opposition parties.

The years from 1945 to 1960 thus brought Turkey's first experiment with a competitive multiparty system. The most important opposition group was the Democratic party (D.P.), formed in 1946 by ex-Premier Celâl Bayar, Adnan Menderes, and other dissident Republicans. In its official program, the D.P. largely confined itself to attacking *étatisme* and promising a more liberal and effective economic policy, but its campaign orators soon fell in with the peasantry's pent-up demand for agricultural developments and for an attenuation of the secularist policy of the Atatürk-Inönü period. The demand for a partial religious restoration was pressed even more vociferously by the Nation party, which had split off from the Democrats in 1948–49.

The three elections of 1950, 1954, and 1957 showed a fairly consistent pattern of alignment (Table 5-3). Voting participation was high—from 75 to 90 percent in each case—a reflection probably as much of the spirit of group solidarity of the peasant majority as of the intensive campaigning by the politicians. The Nation party (renamed the Republican Nation party after its dissolution by court order in 1954, and the Republican Peasant Nation party after its merger with another splinter group in 1958), won only in a single district, Kirşehir in central Anatolia, but in addition attracted a substantial number of votes in some Anatolian small towns and in the poorer districts of Istanbul and Ankara. The Democrats' most consistent backers were the large and medium-sized landowners who benefited most consistently from the Menderes administration's policy of rural development and high cash supports for major crops. The floating vote, which boosted the Democrats' percentage in 1950 and 1954 and substantially reduced it in 1957, was composed of the urban educated groups and of the farmers in some of the poorer agricultural regions who tended to hold the government responsible for good as well as bad crops. The strongholds of the Republican People's party were mainly in eastern Anatolia, including Inönü's home district of Malatya.

Although both major parties courted the industrial workers by promises of legalizing strikes and collective bargaining (promises which neither party made good when in power), most of the labor unions tended to lean to the Democratic party, particularly during its government tenure in the 1950s when more benefits could accrue from administrative action than from opposition oratory. The increasingly repressive policy of the Menderes government caused considerable restlessness in the ranks of his own party, and on one occasion the Premier narrowly escaped being voted out by the party caucus. In 1956, some thirty Democratic deputies seceded in protest against Menderes's restrictive press laws and formed the Liberty party which, like the Nation party,

TABLE 5-3

ELECTIONS IN TURKEY, 1950–1969

Percentage of Vote

	1950	1954	1957	1961	1965	1969
Democratic Party (−1960) ⎱ Justice Party (1961–) ⎰	55	58	48.5	35	53	47
Republican People's Party	40	35	41	37	29	27
Nation Party[a]	5	5	6	14	8	3
New Turkey Party	—	—	—	14	4	1
Other	—	2	4.5	1	6	22[c]
Electoral participation and total seats[b]	89	89	77	82	71	64

Seats in Assembly

	1950	1954	1957	1961	1965	1969
Democratic Party (−1960) ⎱ Justice Party (1961–) ⎰	394	499	421	158	240	256
Republican People's Party	68	31	178	173	134	143
Nation Party[a]	1	5	4	54	42	6
New Turkey Party	—	—	—	65	19	6
Other	10	2	1	—	15	39[c]
Electoral participation and total seats[b]	487	541	610	450	450	450

[a] 1954: Republican Nation Party; 1961: Republican Peasants' Nation Party; 1965: N.P. and R.P.N.P.

[b] The figures for total seats in the 1950s include vacancies caused by candidates being elected from two districts and hence exceed the sum of party seats.

[c] Thereof Reliance Party 7% and 15 seats; Independents 6% and 13 seats.

won only in one province in 1957, and two years later merged with the R.P.P.

During the one-party period, the details of the electoral system were of little practical interest; the slates made up by central R.P.P. headquarters in consultation with the provincial organizations were bound to win by default in any case. (Both the Progressive party of 1924–25 and the Free party of 1930 were formed among dissident R.P.P. members already sitting in the assembly, and neither survived to contest an election.) But with the transition to competitive party politics after 1945, Turkish leaders took a fresh look at their election legislation and eliminated what were felt to be distinctly undemocratic features. Thus in 1946, the voters, who had previously been voting for electors who in turn chose the assemblymen, were allowed to vote for assembly members directly. In 1949, poll watchers from all parties were allowed to supervise the tally, and the courts (rather than the ministry of the interior) were allowed to handle all complaints concerning election irregularities.

Yet some other features of the election system survived until the end of the First Republic in 1960, notably the plurality-list system of voting. Under this system, election districts corresponded to the sixty-odd provinces into which the country is administratively divided, each province electing one assembly member per 40,000 inhabitants. Within each district, the party list obtaining a plurality of votes carried the entire slate of seats—an average of eight to ten seats per province, but as many as thirty or more in the more populous districts such as Istanbul. The system thus corresponded closely to that employed in electing the American presidential electoral college, and, as in the United States, it conferred a heavy premium of seats on the plurality party, inflicting a corresponding penalty on the second party, and a prohibitive penalty on any third or fourth party unless regionally concentrated. As a result, the Democrats in 1950 and 1954 won 85 and 92 per cent, respectively, of the assembly seats on the basis of only 55 and 58 per cent of the vote.

If the multiple-member plurality method of voting created an enormous bias toward a two-party system, the list-method of voting conferred important powers on the party organizations. Within the R.P.P., a majority of nominations was entrusted to the provincial organizations, with a 10 to 20 per cent quota reserved to party headquarters in Ankara. The Democratic party bylaws provided for a similar procedure, except that the entire slates, including provincial nominees, were subject to "approval" by national headquarters—and this in practice meant exclusion of any critics of Premier Menderes from nomination. At first there were a number of safeguards against this heavy concentration of party power: voters could rearrange the order of names on the party lists, substitute new names for the official nominees, or mix various party lists at will, and as a result several districts in 1950 and 1954 returned mixed lists or independent candidates. But by the end of his ten-year reign, Premier Menderes had abolished all these voters' privileges, and in addition secured passage for a law that barred all party dissidents from candidacy. This, in effect, gave Menderes, through his control of the Democratic party central committee, the power to purge his own party at will.

Since much of the dictatorial power which the Democratic party and Menderes personally came to exercise had thus its solid base in the election laws, it was not surprising that the entire system came under sharp attack at the time of the 1960 revolution. The constitution of the Second Republic, adopted in 1961, therefore provided not only for strengthened guarantees of civil rights and of judicial independence but also for a new representative system. The assembly now consists of two chambers, the lower elected by proportional representation and the upper composed mostly of members elected indirectly by the provincial assemblies. The new legislature thus avoided the top-heavy majorities of the 1950s and instead more closely reflected popular opinion. Fears that the new system, as in the Weimar Republic of Germany or the French Fourth Republic, would lead to a wholesale proliferation of parties and to prolonged deadlocks in intervals between short-lived coalition governments have, however, proved groundless—at least up to the early 1970s.

A number of splinter parties indeed emerged, or reemerged, after the interlude of military rule in 1960–61. There was the New Turkey party, improvised in 1960–61 as a successor to the Democrats, which soon lost out in the competition with the Justice party and retained only a limited appeal in the eastern, Turkish-Kurdish portions of the country; there was the religious-conservative Nation party with a number of local strongholds in central Anatolia; there was its offshoot, the Republican Peasants' Nation party, joined after 1961 by the leader of the authoritarian faction of the 1960 military junta, Colonel Alparslan Türkeş, and veering, under his aegis, toward a nationalist and authoritarian position; and there was the Turkish Labor Party, a Marxist group with limited appeal mainly among the Istanbul and Ankara intelligentsia.

But the most notable feature of the 1960s was a reemergence of a two-party alignment—a tribute no doubt to the realism of Turkey's voters and politicians who even in the heat of an election campaign will not entirely forget that from the decision at the polls there must ultimately emerge a single government to rule a single country, that therefore any splintering within a given group invites a victory by its rivals. The major parties of the Second Republic have been the Republican People's party and the Justice party. The R.P.P. is the party of Atatürk and Inönü. It is dedicated to secularism, to a mixed economy with a larger government sector, and to explicit concepts of social and economic planning. One of its besetting problems has been the tension between its educated urban leadership and the rural and underdeveloped character of many of its voting strongholds. Another has been the unwillingness or inability of its grand old man, the octogenarian Inönü, to work with younger associates with strong support in the party organization. (The latest result of this recurrent tension was the formation in 1967 of the Reliance party, which sharply criticized what it considered the parent party's drift toward the socialist left. At the time of its formation, the Reliance party emerged as the third strongest group in parliament, but it soon declined because it failed to build up a correspondingly wide constituency organization in time for the 1969 election.) The Justice party is the chief successor to the Democratic party of Bayar and Menderes. Like its predecessor, it steers a middle-of-the-road course between religious conservatism and secularism, and favors the interests of large and middling landowners as well as of businessmen. Unlike the Democrats, however, the Justice party (since 1965 under the moderate leadership of Demirel) has made its peace with the reforms of the 1960 revolution and with the military establishment. Between them, the R.P.P. and the J.P. have obtained 72 percent of the vote in 1961,

82 percent in 1965, and 74 percent in 1969. Coalition governments formed by the R.P.P. in 1965 gave way to an all-J.P. cabinet supported by a clear majority in both houses.

Political Interest Groups and Political Leadership

Political interest groups in the Western sense of the term are very largely undeveloped in all Middle Eastern political systems except Israel. Instead, a number of institutional groups—foremost being the armies, but also the Muslim ulama, and ethnic groups such as linguistic minorities and nomadic tribes—play important political roles. The vast peasant majority throughout the Middle East is completely unorganized, even where, as in contemporary Turkey, city politicians eagerly solicit their views and votes. In the modern sectors, however, organization is expanding.

Labor and Business

Labor unions have developed in all the "political systems in flux" and in Turkey, but play a relatively insignificant political role. In some cases, they developed spontaneously, but more often their growth has been artificially induced by progressive social legislation patterned since the 1930s on European models. In a situation where only a small percentage of the population is employed in manufacturing, and where vast pools of underemployed recent arrivals or migrants from the villages flood the urban job market, the possibilities for unions to extract concessions from employers through collective bargaining are severely circumscribed. In Egypt, labor demonstrations, supposedly spontaneous but in fact well coordinated, played a major role in consolidating Nasser's power in 1954 and on some subsequent occasions. Generally, in the "systems in flux" labor unions expect to advance their cause through government favor rather than through their own efforts. It follows that independent political action by the unions is rare and inconsequential.

Even in Turkey in the 1950s trade unions would complain that employers circumvented the very generous employment-security and severance-pay provisions of the government's labor code by dismissing their entire work force every six months before these provisions would take effect. More vigorous party competition in the Second Republic, on the other hand, has encouraged a more independent and assertive style of labor politics, following broadly the old A.F. of L. tactic of keeping officially aloof from all parties while rewarding one's friends and punishing one's enemies. The Marxist ideological Turkish Labor party received organized support from only a minority of the unions.

Business interests are an important factor in politics, but they rarely operate through organized pressure-group activity. The prevailing conspiratorial view of both business and politics, the tendency toward state ownership of manufacturing enterprises, and the prominent position within the private sector of foreign-owned oil concerns in the Persian Gulf states and export-import firms throughout the region—all these factors militate against formal associational activity. A business firm is more likely to employ its private connections in the capital to obtain administrative exemption from the multifarious government regulations affecting production and trade than to band together with its competitors to put pressure on parliaments to get the law changed.

Israel is the major exception to this general picture. The Israel Federation of Labor, or Histadruth, plays a preeminent role in the country's politics and economy. Its modern skyscraper office building outside Tel Aviv, popularly known as "the Kremlin," contrasts sharply with the modest converted branch bank' office which long housed the Knesset in Jerusalem, and its annual conventions, which delegates divide along partisan lines into Mapai, Mapam, Mizrahi, and other groups, often forecast important shifts of power in parliament or cabinet.

Army Officers and Students

Among the institutional groups which tend to fill the associational vacuum, the armies—or, more precisely, their officer corps—are by far the most important. The early efforts at modernization in the nineteenth-century Middle East came in response to the impact of Europe's growing military power and uniformly began by reform of the armed services. As a result, army officers were among the first groups in society to become thoroughly committed to modernization, and this made them into a "progressive" force at a later time when society as a whole moved toward modernization. The prevalence of foreign rule and of domestic autocracy and dictatorship in recent Middle Eastern history and the weakness of parliaments, parties, and associational groups all reduced the importance of political decision and change by procedures of debate and instead tended to put a premium on violent change. Army coups and revolutions spearheaded by army officers thus have been a common and recurrent phenomenon throughout the Middle East from the Urabi coup in Egypt in 1881 and the Young Turk revolution of 1908 to the rise of Ataturk and Riza Shah to the wave of Iraqi and Syrian coups of the 1930s and 1940s to the Iraqi revolution of 1958. The sociopolitical role of the army officers in the Middle East in their close association with the interests of a rising urban educated class, thus conforms much more closely to the Bonapartist tradition than to the model of conservative-agrarian Junker militarism.

The role of students in Middle Eastern politics has been not unlike that of the army officers, except that, lacking the physical means of enforcing a new order, they have more often had a merely disruptive effect. The universities, like the armies, have served as focuses of Westernization and recruit an indigenous elite from a broad social and geographic base. The glorification of youth, which has rapidly displaced in Middle Eastern politics the traditional veneration for age, also gives the political expressions of the students an importance beyond their numbers or experience. Since most of them will go into government service of one sort or another, they speak, moreover, in the heady self-assurance of representing tomorrow's governing elite. Thus students at the Istanbul army medical school provided the nucleus of the Young Turk movement in the days of Abdülhamid, and Arab students in Lebanon and at European universities were among the first spokesmen of Arab nationalism in the early years of this century. More recently, the 1960 revolution in Turkey was spearheaded by the university students in Istanbul and Ankara, to be consummated by action of the armed forces.

Traditional Groups

Muslim *ulama,* or learned men (the closest Islamic equivalent to a clergy), play their most entrenched and significant roles in the traditional political systems. Thus the Zaydi-Shii *ulama* of San's used to have the privilege of choosing the Imam's successor from among the deceased incumbent's male relatives, and the Wahhabi *ulama* of al-Riad are consulted about the religious propriety of all major acts of royal legislation. Within the more hierarchical structure of Shii Islam, the *mujtahids* (i.e., the higher grades of Shii *ulama*) still play a distinct corporate role. In the Iraqi cabinets of the monarchical period, one or another *mujtahid* from Karbala was usually represented, and the Iranian constitution of 1905–6 created a council of *mujtahids* to review parliamentary legislation. In the "systems in flux," individual *ulama,* such as the mufti of Jerusalem, Hajj Amin al-Husayni, and Mullah Abu al-Qasim Kashani in Iran, have become the leaders of loosely organized fundamentalist and often terrorist movements of protest against modernization.

The political role of ethnic minorities and of nomadic tribes has already been discussed in an earlier section on social structure. The power of the nomads has sharply declined in recent decades, although they are still a potential force of some moment in southern Iran and in the tribal areas of inland Saudi Arabia. The politics of Lebanon, as we have seen, rests on a careful denominational balance of Christians of various persuasions, of Sunni and Shii Muslims, and of Druzes. The heterogeneous ethnic composition of Iran has given rise to separatist movements, notably the Russian-sponsored Azarbayjan People's Republic of 1945–46, and in Iraq the Kurds of the northern mountains around Sulaymaniyyah and Kirkuk have been a distinctive political force, organized after the 1958 revolution in the Kurdish Democratic party.

Whereas the active role of army officers and of university students is likely to continue in the foreseeable future, it seems safe to say that the political influence of the *ulama* and of ethnic minorities is on the decline. On the other hand, the progress of industrialization and urbanization is leading, in countries like Turkey, Syria, and Iraq, to a proliferation of associational groups—sports societies, study circles, fund-raising societies for the building of new mosques, benevolent societies for migrants to the cities from a given region, etc.—and there is little doubt that these associational groups in the cities, particularly those representing business and labor, will play an increasing role in the future politics of the Middle East.

The Changing Role of Leadership

Little needs to be said about the political leadership of the traditional monarchies. In Afghanistan, Yemen, and Saudi Arabia, leading political positions such as cabinet portfolios remained until recently a virtual monopoly of the princes of the royal house and a few associated tribal or religious leaders. In the "systems in flux," on the other hand, an older conservative leadership must be distinguished from the revolutionary leadership that seeks to replace it. The more traditional leaders, who still predominate in Iran and Jordan and who controlled Iraq until 1958, include mainly large landowners and members of the traditional urban upper class whose record of public service goes back for several generations or even centuries. Within the rising elite, journalists, lawyers, schoolteachers, engineers, and other Western-educated members of the professions are prominent.

Army officers have held an important place in both the older and newer elites, as the examples of Nuri al-Said and the Abd al-Karim Qasim in Iraq well illustrate. In part, the conflict between the two leadership groups is one between generations, the defenders of the established order being mostly men in their fifties and sixties, the advocates of drastic change in their thirties and forties. (Muhammad Musaddiq, who as a septuagenarian led the abortive Iranian revolution of 1951–53, is a rare exception.) This age factor means that the younger generation's revolutionary urge is tempered by the awareness that they are bound to move into power through mere passage of time. It also means that young radicals may lose their exuberant enthusiasm for change by the time they achieve power through peaceful or forceful means and have come to enjoy it during some lucrative years in office. Nuri al-Said was a young lieutenant in his late twenties when he prominently joined the nationalist movement to erect an Iraqi state upon the ruins of the Ottoman Empire; forty years later he had become the symbol of the corrupt established order, which younger Iraqis would confidently have expected to crumble upon Nuri's retirement for ill health, even if he had not met his violent death in the 1958 revolution.

All political leadership performs a function of mediation—mediation among the conflicting aspirations of politically articulate citizens, mediation between the traditional foundations of politics and an emerging new order, mediation between a country's limited resources of political power and its ambitions for international prestige, mediation, most generally, between aspiration and reality. At difficult periods of transition—from foreign or dynastic rule to nationhood, from a traditional agrarian, religious order to a modern urban, industrial society—this task of mediation involves many complex, rapid, and fateful decisions. Such periods of swift and fundamental transition therefore generally require strong personal leadership, an arrangement which heightens the chances of both success and failure. Successful leadership depends not only on the leader's sagacity in assessing the real situation and its potentialities for the future and on his ability to symbolize in a coherent fashion the diverse hopes of his followers. It also hinges on his ability to select subordinate leaders who can assist him in his task and from among whom a successor will emerge when the original leader passes from the scene.

The Middle Eastern setting of the last half century has made extraordinary demands on leadership in the transition from traditional Muslim to modern technological civilization, in the groping for a new sense of national identity, in the precarious foreign policy maneuvers of a weak and divided region located at the point of intersection of important interests of many of the world's most powerful countries. Some leaders have acquitted themselves of their tasks magnificently—Atatürk in persuading his Turkish countrymen to forsake imperial ambitions and to concentrate their energies on the development of a smaller, national territory; Ben Gurion in giving coherence and momentum to a new state founded by persecuted immigrants. But it should not be forgotten that in their case half the secret of leadership turned out to be followership—the willingness of Turks and of Israelis to join in disciplined purposeful political organization. Gamal Abdul Nasser of Egypt has had a far more varied record of achievement and of failure: his overambitious foreign policy has been in sharp contrast to Atatürk's conscious self-limitation, and Egypt's overpopulation has prevented any dramatic economic progress. Still, considering these adverse conditions and recalling the career of Nasser's predecessors in Egypt and contemporaries in other Arab countries, it is remarkable that his regime has managed to provide political continuity in Egypt for already close to two decades. Muhammad Riza Shah's political survival through the crises of the 1940s and 1950s, and the growing success of his "white revolution" of the 1960s are equally remarkable; and the courage and skill with which King Husayn of Jordan has managed to cling to his throne—providing the only point of coherence in an artificially contrived state—is perhaps the most remarkable of all. Elsewhere in the Middle East, there has been a similar emphasis on personal leadership, but in the absence of settled political institutions, stable cultural settings, or accepted notions of national identity, this leadership has been ineffectual, and subject to sudden kaleidoscopic shifts—it has remained a rhetorical claim unsupported by political performance.

The preceding discussion of the dynamic elements in Middle Eastern politics—of parties, elections, and interest groups—throws into sharp relief the vast range of differences among the several countries. Many factors of traditional religion, social structure, and culture are common to the entire region, and these forces still are supreme in Yemen, Afghanistan, and Saudi Arabia. The modernizing forces of political organization and agitation, of reform and revolution, which have barely begun to impinge on the traditional monarchies, are more fully at work in the "systems in flux"; the forces of tradition are still in uneasy control in Iran and Jordan, those of revolution are triumphant in Egypt and Iraq, whereas Syria shifts back and forth among various points of the spectrum. Only in Turkey and especially in Israel have stable forms of political organization emerged. It goes without saying that the operation of formal governmental institutions is profoundly affected by these differences of political dynamics.

Chapter *6*

Decision-Making

THE ORGANS OF
GOVERNMENT

The Middle East, as we have seen, was among the earliest parts of the non-European world to adopt the Western custom of written constitutions, and the influence of particular European models, such as that of the Belgian Constitution of 1831 on the Ottoman fundamental law of 1876, is palpable. The early enthusiasm for codified constitutions arose in the optimistic minds of nineteenth-century reformers who, with a few decisive legal changes, hoped to cure the evils of autocracy, of social backwardness, of economic insolvency, and of military weakness. The immediate sequence of events, however, led to rapid disillusionment. The proclamation of the Ottoman Constitution of 1876 was followed within the year by renewed defeat at the hands of Russia and, in 1881, by the institution of a European-controlled administration for the Ottoman public debt. In Egypt, the constitutionalist movement of 1881–82 was thwarted in its embryonic stage by the British occupation of the country. And in Iran, the constitutional revolution of 1905–6 foundered against partitions from abroad and coups from within.

Even aside from these foreign complications, the new constitutional precepts were more easily promulgated than implemented. At times, the constitution as a whole or essential parts of it were simply ignored. Abdulhamid's prorogation of the new Ottoman Parliament in 1878—as it turned out, for thirty years—is a glaring example. Similarly, in Iran the upper chamber envisaged by the 1905–6 Constitution was only convened as late as 1949. More basically, the absence of voluntary associations and of deeply rooted, stable party organizations made the purposeful operation of institutions of parliamentary government difficult or impossible. The experience of the Ottoman Empire after 1908 demonstrated how quickly the universal hopes for a liberal constitutional order could be converted into the ugly reality of a partisan and military dictatorship. Throughout the 1920s and 1930s, the proclamations of parliamentary supremacy contained in the fundamental laws did not prevent the preponderance of the French mandate administration in Syria and of the clique around King Faysal and General Nuri in Iraq, around Riza Shah in Iran, and around Kemal and his People's party in Turkey.

The number of countries without formal constitution has steadily been diminishing. Afghanistan adopted a constitution in 1931 which, however, was never implemented. Instead, the government remained in the hands of the king (Muhammad Zahir Shah since 1933), with most key ministerial positions held by his immediate relatives. A more genuine effort at constitutionalism was made in 1964, and the new fundamental law specifically prohibits princes from holding posts in the cabinet or other high office. Instead, wide-reaching powers are vested in a bicameral parliament, with an elected lower and a royally appointed upper house. In Yemen, the absolute rule of the king, once one of the world's most traditional rulers, gave way, in the republican regime of 1962, to a succession of military rulers. The republicans only adopted a provisional constitution which, however, underwent frequent amendment as a result of shifting governments and shifting fortunes in the civil war.

This leaves two major countries without constitution—Saudi Arabia at one end of the spectrum, and Israel at the other. In Saudi Arabia, in theory, the ruler's will is supreme within the confines of traditional Islamic law. In practice, a law concerning the organization of the cabinet defines much of formal government organization, and the flood of oil revenues, under Kink Faysal's more purposeful administration, has given rise to an expanding bureaucracy. In Israel, a combination of British tradition and of objections by the orthodox rabbinate has prevented the adoption of a formal written constitution, although the unwritten constitution based on parliamentary cabinet government and civil liberties is strongly entrenched. All other countries—Egypt, Jordan, Iraq, Syria, Lebanon, Yemen, Iran, and Turkey—have had written constitutions which they operate with varying success. The experience with the Menderes dictatorship in Turkey—based on a constitution providing for strong legislative supremacy, an electoral law heavily weighted in favor of the plurality party, and party bylaws giving extensive powers to the top leader—has given rise, as we have seen, to a thorough constitutional reexamination; and the constitution for the Second Republic provides for such safeguards against concentration of power as bicameralism, judicial review, proportional representation, and a detailed codification of civil rights.

In Iran and Jordan, the written provisions for constitutional monarchy lead a precarious existence amid the realities of royal prerogative and revolutionary popular ferment. In Lebanon, the parliamentary republican constitution has operated fairly smoothly, with occasional interruptions such as those in 1952 and 1958; the real balance of the political system is provided by the recognition on all sides that toleration and a modicum of cooperation among the rival denominations are essential to the country's commercial prosperity.

The United Arab Republic Constitution of March 5, 1958, contained a large number of declamatory provisions attesting to the nationalist and social-reformist convictions of its sponsors (e.g., Article 1: ". . . its people are a part of the Arab nation"; Article 3: "Social solidarity is the basis of society"; Article 6: "Social justice is the basis for the levying of taxes and for public expenditures"). But the constitution was conveniently vague as to the structure of governmental machinery (Article 13: "Legislative power is exercised by the National Assembly. A decree of the President of the Republic will determine the number of its members and the manner of their selection . . ."). In contrast to other dictatorships which prevent the formation of rival parties in practice rather than in theory, a decree by President Nasser, issued one week after the U.A.R. Constitution went into effect (although it was earlier in operation in Egypt) prohibited all political parties with the exception of the officially sponsored "National Union."

Beneath this top layer of varied formal institutions there is a fair degree of uniformity of administrative structure and procedure. The local administration is usually patterned on the French model, with prefects appointed from the central Interior Ministry. The judiciary is not formally separated from the rest of the administration—courts are part of the Ministry of Justice much as tax bureaus are of the Ministry of Finance. Although judges usually are irremovable, punitive transfers and compulsory retirements limit their independence. The armed forces under the chief of staff usually play an independent role within or vis-à-vis the government, even where they are nominally subordinated to a civilian minister of defense. The religious establishment is paid from public funds. Except for Turkey, where secular legislation has been in effect since the 1920s, religious authorities still define and administer the law of marriage and inheritance—even in Israel. Education is public and secular and its administration centralized. All in all, the notorious instability and radicalism of Middle Eastern politics have been mitigated by a remarkable degree of administrative conservatism and continuity.

Chapter *7*

GOVERNMENTAL
PERFORMANCE

Any reasoned evaluation of governmental performance must make explicit the standards of judgment to be applied. It used to be fashionable in the West, and particularly in the United States, to assume that democracy, being based on "self-evident truths," was the natural form of government which could be expected to come into existence automatically as soon as the restraints of dynastic absolutism or colonial rule were removed. (Much in the same vein, nineteenth-century liberal economists assumed that individual initiative freed from government control would be guided by the "unseen hand" of a benevolent if secularized Providence to ensure prosperity and welfare for the community at large.) On the basis of such conceptions, it would be easy to become indignant at governments of the Middle East (or, for that matter of other parts of Asia, Africa, or Latin America) for their inexcusable laggardness in attaining a full flowering of democratic liberties and free-enterprise prosperity. Such a judgment would be as irrelevant as the underlying axioms are naive.

We have come to realize in the twentieth century that representative institutions, more perhaps than any other form of government, are the product of gradual evolution and of special historical circumstances. Thus, in Western Europe, the basic task of national unification was accomplished in painful struggles from the thirteenth to the seventeenth centuries, and the administrative structure of modern states evolved under the absolute monarchs who reigned from the sixteenth to the eighteenth centuries, long before legislative control and popular elections became the order of the day. In the Middle East, the quest for basic national identity and for countrywide systems of administration is still a major item on the political agenda—at a time when the populations in most of the states already are impatient for the tangible benefits of social welfare and economic progress.

A more realistic assessment of the performance of Middle Eastern governmental systems must consider in turn the establishment of new states, the assertion and maintenance of their independence, the expansion of governmental and administrative functions, and, finally, their accomplishments in the economic and social spheres. Above all, we must not forget how recent a creation the present Middle Eastern state system is. As late as 1914, Syria and Iraq were mere geographic concepts; Jordan was the name only of the river and as a country not even a geographic concept; Turkey was a European misnomer for the Ottoman Empire. Egypt retained its distinct geographic identity but was *de facto* part of the British and *de jure* part of the Ottoman Empire. Arabia was a congeries of amirates, shaykhdoms, and tribal confederations among which the Saudi was one of the lesser. What was to become Israel was a utopian dream in the minds of a handful of absentee Zionist enthusiasts. Only Iran and Afghanistan had had a political identity dating back several centuries. The most remarkable achievement of most Middle Eastern states, then, is that they have managed to become established and to maintain themselves in existence as recognizable political entities at all.

Maintenance of political identity has involved a struggle in two directions—against internal forces of disruption and against outside threats to independence. Some of the countries of the region have registered their most solid achievements in the field of internal unification. The Kurdish mountaineers, who were a disruptive force defiant of any outside government as late as the 1920s, have been fully subdued and integrated in Turkey but continue to pose a serious challenge in Iraq. The tribes of the Arabian peninsula were unified and subjected to government control— often for the first time in history—by the concerted efforts of Ibn Saud and the Wahhabi religious brotherhood. And Israel has imbued a polyglot mass of immigrants with a common national purpose and sentiment. Even Lebanon, faced with a precarious seesaw balance of Christians and Muslims, has found unity in an institutionalized pluralism. Only Jordan notably lacks in national integration, making the survival of state and dynasty amid the swirling crosscurrents of Middle Eastern politics all the more notable an accomplishment.

The external independence of Middle Eastern countries has been attained and maintained more often by good fortune than by the countries' own efforts. Only Turkey and Israel owe their statehood to wars of independence, and these two wars were fought only against comparatively weak local antagonists. The termination of Ottoman rule over Arabs was achieved mainly by force of British arms, and it was the exhaustion of Britain and France in their war with Germany and Japan in 1939–45 which effectively undermined European hegemony. More recently, the rivalry between the United States and Russia has turned out to be the most effective guarantee of the independence of the states of the Middle East. Each superpower has tended to shield the area from domination by the other, and both jointly have warded off aggressive interference by smaller powers, such as the concerted Israeli-French-British attack on Egypt in 1956. It remains to be seen whether growing Soviet influence since the 1967 war will fundamentally upset this long-time balance.

Within the boundaries of these new Middle Eastern states, there has been a steady growth of governmental function and administrative machinery. In the Ottoman Empire of the mid-nineteenth century, some 90 per cent of public revenues were expended on the armed forces, the civil list, and the servicing of the mounting public debt. The ruler's power, though all-encompassing in theory, hardly extended beyond his palace and capital and rarely reached into the daily lives of his subjects. Today, by contrast, universal military training, universal public education, extensive public works programs, and a wide array of economic controls, individual income taxes and social welfare legislation, state-owned transportation networks and broadcasting systems have given modern governments, in all but the most traditional states, a power and a responsibility over the daily lives of the citizenry beyond the wildest dreams of nineteenth-century sultans or shahs. And although corruption and partisan repression are common phenomena, a growing elite of civil servants with a modern, Western education are administering this vast network of government functions with increasing dedication and competence. The principle that government is the servant of the people and that it should be representative of their aspirations is accepted without theoretical challenge in nearly all countries of the region, finding increasing acceptance even in Saudi Arabia, Afghanistan, and Yemen.

The governments' practical possibilities to serve their publics are circumscribed by ill-trained manpower, by the highy uneven distribution of economic resources among the countries of the region, and by exploding populations with soaring expectations. Of the countries of the Middle East, Turkey was the fortunate heir to the late Ottoman Empire's pool of administrative manpower—army officers, judges, district administrators, teachers—roughly nine-tenths of which stayed in the Turkish Republic, with the remainder dividing mainly between Syria and Iraq. Israel, too, has been fortunate in being able to count on the superior skills and dedication of early Jewish immigrants from Central and Eastern Europe who prepared the state for the subsequent absorption of masses of immigrants from the Middle East.

Elsewhere, administrative systems had to be created in the almost total absence of trained or experienced personnel. It is symbolic that, whereas the Turkish Republic was founded by Mustafa Kemal, who had risen to the rank of brigadier general in the Ottoman army, the new Iraqi state was formed by a group of officers who had been lieutenants or captains before joining Amir Faysal's liberation army. Even in Turkey, the traditional ethnic division of labor, which relegated the trades and professions to non-Muslims, left a noticeable gap in the middle-class occupations once power shifted to the Muslim majority. Throughout the area, there remains a severe shortage of doctors, engineers, accountants, and other technicians of economic development. Although increasing numbers of these are graduated from indigenous institutions of higher learning—especially in Turkey and more recently in Iran—there is still heavy reliance on study abroad (in Europe, the United States, and more recently Russia) or at the foreign colleges in the area (such as the American University of Beirut and Robert College in Istanbul).

The rapid increase in oil royalties received by Kuwayt, Saudi Arabia, Iran, and Iraq has made available monetary resources for economic development which would have surpassed the wildest dreams of previous generations. Foreign aid—mainly from the United States government to Turkey and Iran, from Britain to Jordan, from the U.S.S.R. to Iraq and Afghanistan, and from private United States sources (mainly the United Jewish Appeal) to Israel—has added equally sizable amounts. Yet a variety of factors limits the economic effectiveness of this capital inflow—the lack of natural resources other than oil in Kuwayt and Saudi Arabia, widespread governmental corruption in Iran, lack of planning and coordination in Turkey. Dedicated and skilled leadership in the political, economic, and technical fields still tends to be the scarcest resource, and it is in this respect most particularly that Israel excels among the countries of the Middle East.

Chapter *8*

PROBLEMS AND
PROSPECTS

In assessing the forces for change in Middle Eastern politics, we must accord a crucial place to the uncertainties of the international situation. The Middle East has long been a crossroads of power conflict, from the days of Darius, Alexander, and Pompey to those of Napoleon, Eisenhower, and Khrushchev. Its transportation routes, once important for the silk and spice trade or as part of the British Empire's "lifeline to India," today convey a steady stream of petroleum from the wells of the Persian Gulf region to the furnaces and fuel tanks of Europe. In the cold war between Russia and the West, the Middle East has held an important strategic position, first as a barrier to Soviet expansion toward the Mediterranean, the Indian Ocean, and Africa, and recently as a testing ground for the appeal of the Communist versus the Western socioeconomic orders to rapidly modernizing states and peoples.

With the shift of global military strategy from bombers to missiles the alignment of this or that piece of territory in the pattern of military alliances has become less important. But international crises have focused on the Middle East at regular intervals—Azerbayjan in 1945–46, Palestine in 1948, Iranian oil in 1951, Suez in 1954 and 1956, Lebanon, Jordan, and Iraq in 1958, Yemen in 1962, and most recently the third Israeli-Arab war of 1967 with its overtones of American-Russian confrontation. Western imperial positions have irretrievably been relinquished; even in the Persian Gulf, British military withdrawal was scheduled for 1971. But a Soviet take-over in one or another country, whether through internal revolt followed by military occupation or through increasingly closer cooperation with indigenous leaders, remains a possibility which would change the domestic political picture of the affected country thoroughly and pose a novel threat to its neighbors.

But even aside from these external complications, much international ferment is generated within the Middle East itself. Although a peace of sorts between Israel and her Arab neighbors was restored after the military clashes of 1948, 1956, and 1967 the *de facto* peace has become more precarious each time.

Among the Arab states, the borders drawn as part of the European-imposed settlement of the First World War enjoy no respect, and political loyalties continue to be divided between existing states and the unrealized ideal of a wider Arab nation-state. Recurrent territorial claims and conflicts have been the result—along the Yemen-Aden border, around the Buraymi Oasis, over Kuwayt, and elsewhere. The Egyptian-Syrian merger of 1958 has been the only tangible step so far toward Arab unification, and the dissolution of that union in 1961 has taken much of the impetus out of the Arab unification drive of the 1950s. It seems likely that the Arab countries will become increasingly conscious of their separate identities, although any major internal change of regime in any of the countries (such as the collapse of monarchy in Yemen or Jordan) might present the question in a new form. Needless to say, any basic realignment of borders without will drastically alter the operation of the political process within. In view of the abundance of oil income in Kuwayt, Saudi Arabia, Iraq, and the smaller Persian Gulf territories (in contrast to the economic poverty and over-population of states like Egypt and Jordan), the socioeconomic consequences of any sweeping realignment will be equally profound.

International complications, border revisions, and possible mergers apart, it seems safe to predict that the combined operation of political and social pressures will transform political processes in Yemen and Afghanistan, making them increasingly resemble those countries we have called "political systems in flux." In this latter category, it seems likely that the monarchic-oligarchic systems of Jordan, Saudi Arabia, and Iran will sooner or later (and perhaps in that sequence) be threatened by the type of revolution that swept away the monarchy in Egypt in 1952, in Iraq in 1958, and in Libya in 1969—and that already came close to success in Iran in 1953 and in Jordan in the late fifties.

In the postrevolutionary regimes of Egypt-U.A.R. and Iraq, there has been a remarkable parallelism of political dynamics. A period of vigorous suppression of representatives of the *ancien régime* has been followed by a gradual diversification of the support of the military dictatorship; promises of socioeconomic reform have alternated with ambitious manifestations of an expansionist foreign policy, and periods of close cooperation in international affairs with the Soviet Union have alternated with a more realistic assessment of the dangers of Communist imperialism and to a more genuinely neutralist course. In the absence of other yardsticks, similar developments may be envisaged for any future postrevolutionary regimes in Jordan, Iran, and Saudi Arabia. For some time, in any case, the choice of domestic regime for most Middle Eastern countries seems to lie between conservative, pseudoconstitutional oligarchy and attempts at social revolution under auspices of a military or party dictatorship. Genuinely democratic institutions are solidly entrenched only in Israel. In Turkey, after the initial false start under Menderes in the 1950s, they have begun to strike root in the second Republic of the 1960s.

BIBLIOGRAPHY

Middle East, General

The Cambridge History of Islam. 2 vols. Cambridge, England: Cambridge University Press, 1970.

Campbell, John C., Defense of the Middle East. 2nd ed. New York: Harper & Row, Publishers, 1960.

Coon, Carleton S., Caravan: The Story of the Middle East, rev. ed. New York: Holt, Rinehart & Winston, Inc., 1961.

Fisher, Sydney N., ed., The Military in Middle Eastern Society and Politics. Columbus: Ohio State University Press, 1963.

————, Social Forces in the Middle East. Ithaca, N.Y.: Cornell University Press, 1955.

Frye, Richard N., ed., Islam and the West. The Hague and New York: Gregory Lounz, 1957.

Halpern, Manfred, The Politics of Social Change in the Middle East and North Africa. Princeton, N.J.: Princeton University Press, 1963.

Hurewitz, J. C., Diplomacy in the Near and Middle East. 2 vols. New York: Van Nostrand Reinhold Company, 1956.

————, Middle East Politics: The Military Dimension. New York: Frederick A. Praeger, Inc., 1969.

————, The Struggle for Palestine. New York: W. W. Norton & Company, Inc., 1950.

Issawi, Charles, ed., The Economic History of the Middle East, 1800–1914: A Book of Readings. Chicago: University of Chicago Press, 1966.

Kirk, George E., A Short History of the Middle East, 6th ed. New York: Frederick A. Praeger, Inc., 1960.

Laqueur, Walter Z., Communism and Nationalism in the Middle East. New York: Frederick A. Praeger, Inc., 1956.

Lenczowski, George, The Middle East in World Affairs, 2nd ed. Ithaca, N.Y.: Cornell University Press, 1956.

————, Oil and State in the Middle East. Ithaca, N.Y.: Cornell University Press, 1960.

Lerner, Daniel et al., The Passing of Traditional Society. New York: The Free Press, 1958.

The Middle East Journal. Washington, D.C., 1947– (quarterly).

Nolte, Richard H., ed., The Modern Middle East. New York: Atherton Press, Inc., 1963.

Proctor, J. Harris, ed., Islam and International Relations. New York: Frederick A. Praeger, Inc., 1965.

Rivlin, Benjamin, and Joseph Szyliowicz, eds., The Contemporary Middle East. New York: Random House, Inc., 1965.

Rustow, Dankwart A., Politics and Westernization in the Near East. Princeton, N.J.: Center of International Studies, 1956.

————, "The Politics of the Near East," in G. A. Almond and J. S. Coleman, eds., The Politics of the Developing Areas. Princeton, N.J.: Princeton University Press, 1960.

Smith, Wilfred Cantwell, Islam in Modern History. Princeton, N.J.: Princeton University Press, 1957.

Von Grunebaum, Gustave E., Modern Islam: The Search for Cultural Identity. Berkeley, Calif.: University of California Press, 1962.

Afghanistan

Sykes, Sir Percy M., *A History of Afghanistan*. New York: The Macmillan Company, 1940.

Wilber, Donald N., *Afghanistan*. New York: Taplinger Publishing Co., Inc., 1956.

Arab Countries

Antonius, George, *The Arab Awakening*. Philadelphia: J. B. Lippincott Co., 1938.

Berger, Morroe, *The Arab World Today*. Garden City, N.Y.: Doubleday & Company, Inc., 1962.

Haim, Sylvia, ed., *Arab Nationalism*. Berkeley, Calif.: University of California Press, 1962.

Hourani, Albert H., *Syria and Lebanon*. London: Oxford University Press, 1946.

————, *Arabic Thought in the Liberal Age*. London: Oxford University Press, 1961.

Issawi, Charles, *Egypt in Revolution*. London: Oxford University Press, 1963.

Kedourie, Elie, *England and the Middle East, 1913–1920*. London: Bowes & Bowes Ltd., 1956.

Kerr, Malcolm H., *The Arab Cold War, 1958–1967*, 2nd ed. London: Oxford University Press, 1967.

Khadduri, Majid, *Independent Iraq, 1932–1951*, 2nd ed. London: Oxford University Press, 1960.

Landes, David S., *Bankers and Pashas*. Cambridge: Harvard University Press, 1958.

Longrigg, Stephen H., *Syria and Lebanon under French Mandate*. London: Oxford University Press, 1958.

————, and Frank Stoakes, *Iraq*. New York: Frederick A. Praeger, Inc., 1959.

McDonald, Robert W., *The League of Arab States*. Princeton, N.J.: Princeton University Press, 1965.

Nasser, Gamal Abdul, *Egypt's Liberation: The Philosophy of the Revolution*. Washington, D.C.: Public Affairs Press, 1953.

Nuseibeh, Hazem Zaki, *The Ideas of Arab Nationalism*. Ithaca, N.Y.: Cornell University Press, 1956.

Safran, Nadav, *Egypt in Search of Political Community*. Cambridge: Harvard University Press, 1961.

Iran

Banani, Amin, *The Modernization of Iran, 1921–1941*. Stanford, Calif.: Stanford University Press, 1961.

Binder, Leonard, *Iran: Political Development in a Changing Society*. Berkeley, Calif.: University of California Press, 1962.

Browne, Edward G., *The Persian Revolution*. Cambridge, England: Cambridge University Press, 1910.

Cottam, Richard W., *Nationalism in Iran*. Pittsburgh: University of Pittsburgh Press, 1964.

Keddie, Nikki R., *Religion and Rebellion in Iran*. London: Frank Cass & Co., Ltd., 1966.

Lenczowski, George, *Russia and the West in Iran*. Ithaca, N.Y.: Cornell University Press, 1949.

Upton, Joseph M., *The History of Modern Iran*. Cambridge, Mass.: Harvard University Press, 1960.

Wilber, Donald N., *Iran: Past and Present*, 4th ed. Princeton, N.J.: Princeton University Press, 1958.

Israel

Fein, Leonard J., *Politics in Israel*. Boston: Little, Brown and Company, 1967.

Halpern, Ben, *The Idea of a Jewish State*. Cambridge, Mass.: Harvard University Press, 1961.

Safran, Nadav, *The United States and Israel*. Cambridge, Mass.: Harvard University Press, 1963.

Weizmann, Chaim, *Trial and Error*. New York: Harper & Row, Publishers, 1949.

Turkey

Berkes, Niyazi, *The Development of Secularism in Turkey*. Montreal: McGill University Press, 1964.

Davison, Roderic H., *Reform in the Ottoman Empire, 1856–1876*. Princeton, N.J.: Princeton University Press, 1963.

Frey, Frederick W., *The Turkish Political Elite*. Cambridge, Mass.: The M.I.T. Press, 1965.

Hershlag, Z. Y., Turkey: *An Economy in Transition*, 2nd ed. The Hague: Mouton & Co., 1967.

Karpat, Kemal H., *Turkey's Politics: The Transition to a Multi-party System*. Princeton, N.J.: Princeton University Press, 1959.

Kinross [Patrick Balfour], Lord, *Atatürk, the Rebirth of a Nation*. London: George Weidenfeld & Nicolson Ltd., 1964.

Lewis, Bernard, *The Emergence of Modern Turkey*. London: Oxford University Press, 1961.

Ramsaur, E. E., Jr., *The Young Turks*. Princeton, N.J.: Princeton University Press, 1957.

Rustow, Dankwart A., "Atatürk as Founder of a State," in D. A. Rustow, ed., *Philosophers and Kings*. New York: George Braziller, Publishers, 1970.

Shorter, Frederic C., ed., *Four Studies on the Development of Turkey*. London: Frank Cass & Co., Ltd., 1967.

Ward, Robert E., and Dankwart A. Rustow, eds., *Political Modernization in Japan and Turkey*. Princeton, N.J.: Princeton University Press, 1964.

Weiker, Walter F., *The Turkish Revolution, 1960–1961*. Washington, D.C.: The Brookings Institution, 1962.

APPENDIX

TABLE I

COMPARATIVE TABLE OF NATIONAL POPULATIONS, AREAS,
EDUCATIONAL ATTAINMENT, AND CIRCULATION OF MASS MEDIA

| | DEMOGRAPHY | | | | AREA AND POPULA- | |
Country	Population (in thousands) 1947	1967	Annual population increase 1958–63	1963–67	Total area (in thousands of sq. km.)	Inhabitants per sq. km.
	(1)	*(2)*	*(3)*	*(4)*	*(5)*	*(6)*
Afghanistan	12,000	15,751	2.8%	2.0%	647.5	24
Egypt (U.A.R.)	19,088	30,907	2.5	2.5	1,001.4	31
Iran	17,000	26,284	2.4	3.1	1,648.0	16
Iraq	4,800	8,440	1.6	2.5	434.9	19
Israel	657[a]	2,669	3.5	2.9	20.7	129
Jordan	—	2,039	2.9	3.3	97.7	21
Kuwayt	120	520	10.7	7.6	16.0	33
Lebanon	1,179	2,520	3.0	2.5	10.4	242
Masqat and Uman	830	565	0.5	—	212.4	3
Persian Gulf Federation						
Bahrayn	—	193	2.8	3.2	0.6	323
Qatar	—	75	6.6	8.1	22.0	3
Trucial Shaykhdoms	—	180	3.0	—	83.6	2
Saudi Arabia	6,000	6,990	1.9	1.7	2,149.7	3
Southern Yemen	—	1,170	—	2.2	287.7	4
Aden	—	—	—	—	—	—
South Arabia	—	—	—	—	—	—
Syria	3,662[b]	5,570	4.2	2.9	185.2	30
Turkey	19,250	32,710	2.9	2.5	767.2	42
Yemen	7,000	5,000	2.6	—	195.0	26
India	338,727	511,125	2.3	2.5	3,268.1	156
Japan	80,216[a]	99,918	0.9	1.0	369.8	270
USSR	193,000	235,520	1.7	1.2	22,402.2	11
USA	144,034	199,118	1.6	1.3	9,363.4	21

[a] 1948 (Israel: Jewish population only)
[b] 1946
[c] 1960
[d] 1964
[e] 1965
[f] 1966
[g] 1956
[h] This is the so-called "adjusted school enrollment ratio," i.e., primary and secondary school attendance as percentage of population in the corresponding age groups—allowing

| TION DENSITY (1967) | | EDUCATION AND COMMUNICATION | | | | | | |
Arable area (in thousands of sq. km.)	Inhabitants per sq. km. of arable area	Literacy rate ca. 1960	School enrollment[h] 1950	School enrollment[h] 1964	Newspaper circulation[i] (per thousand inhabitants) 1952	Newspaper circulation[i] (per thousand inhabitants) 1965	Radio sets (per thousand inhabitants) 1950	Radio sets (per thousand inhabitants) 1965
(7)	(8)	(9)	(10)	(11)	(12)	(13)	(14)	(15)
78.4	201	—	3%	10%	1	6	0.7	13
28.0	1,103	19.5%	25	51	—	—	13	54
115.9c	174	12.8g	16	40	7	—	11k	68
75.0d	93	14.5	18	58	20	12j	6	349
4.1	649	84.2	73	83	167	148j	122	290
11.4e	167	32.4	27	73	12	8	2	136
0.03	17,333	46.8	21	101	—	3j	—	411d
3.1	823	—	47	81	2	8	2	12c
—	—	—	—	—	—	—	—	—
—	—	—	—	—	—	—	—	—
—	—	—	—	—	—	—	—	—
3.7e	1,751	—	2	12	—	—	—	—
2.5f	464	—	—	—	—	—	11	268
—	—	—	22	46	—	—	—	—
—	—	—	5	14	—	—	—	—
61.3	91	29.6	35	46	19	21d	15	329
262.5	121	38.1	33	55	31	51c	17	79
—	—	—	11	9	—	—	—	—
1,624.3d	230	27.8	21	41	7	13	1	11
57.5	1,739	97.8	86	85	374	451	111	209
2,420.0	96	98.5	83	100	109	264	61	320
1,764.4d	109	97.8	100	105	342	310	560	1,233

for differences among countries as to normal school starting age and years of school. Pupils starting before or finishing after the normal age account for the figures in excess of 100.

[i] This includes daily general-interest newspapers.

[j] 1962

[k] 1963

Sources

Col. 1–4, 6, 14–15: United Nations, *Statistical Yearbook.*

Col. 5: United Nations, *Demographic Yearbook.*

Col. 7–8: *FAO Production Yearbook.*

Col. 9–13: UNESCO, *Statistical Yearbook.*

TABLE II

ECONOMIC DEVELOPMENT AND DEFENSE SPENDING

Country	GNP per capita (U.S. dollars), 1966	DISTRIBUTION OF LABOR FORCE				Defense expenditure per capita (U.S. dollars), 1965	Per capita energy consumption (kg.), 1967	Per capital crude steel consumption (kg.), 1967	Cement production (thousands of metric tons), 1967
		Year	Primary sector[b]	Secondary sector[c]	Tertiary sector[d]				
	(1)		(2)	(3)	(4)	(5)	(6)	(7)	(8)
Afghanistan	104[a]	—	—	—	—	1.92	27	—	37
Egypt (U.A.R.)	168	1960	56.6%	11.3%	29.2%[e]	15.60	267	24	2,629[g]
Iran	252	1966	41.8	23.7	23.2	13.48	451	51	1,538
Iraq	268	1957	47.9	14.2	24.9	32.92	610	28	1,279[g]
Israel	1,454	1968	10.9	33.8	52.6	121.50	2,262	118	805
Jordan	266	1961	35.3	21.1	25.2	29.40	265	—	321
Kuwait	3,462	1965	1.1	29.1	66.5	153.50	6,648	—	—
Lebanon	476	—	—	—	—	12.23	648	89	1,016
Masqat and Uman	—	—	—	—	—	—	32	—	—
Persian Gulf Federation									
Bahrayn	—	1968	8.7	16.7	61.6	—	3,601	—	—
Qatar	—	—	—	—	—	—	1,400	—	—
Trucial Shaykhdoms	—	—	—	—	—	—	338	—	—
Saudi Arabia	380	—	—	—	—	40.93	440	22	410
Southern Yemen	—	1958	—	40.2	33.3	—	2,023	—	—
Syria	201	1967	58.1	13.0	23.5	17.05	393	30	688
Turkey	279[a]	1965	71.8	10.3	14.7	3.02	422	24	4,236
Yemen	103	—	—	—	—	14.02	10	—	—
India	74	1961	72.9	11.1	14.8	2.79[g]	176	13	11,309
Japan	986	1965	24.3	31.9	42.4	9.46[g]	2,323	513	42,494
USSR	1,531	1959	35.9	33.6[f]	18.0	201.63[g]	3,957	415	84,809
USA	3,796	1968	4.9	32.7	57.6	321.36[g]	9,828	634	64,449

[a] 1965

[b] Includes agriculture, hunting, fishing, and forestry.

[c] Includes mining, manufacturing, and construction.

[d] Includes trade, utilities, finance, communications, and services.

[e] Figures do not add to 100% because of "other" and "unemployed" categories.

[f] Includes transportation and communications workers.

[g] 1966

Sources

Col. 1, 5: US Arms Control and Disarmament Agency, *World-wide Military Expenditures and Related Data, Calendar Year 1965* and *Calendar Year 1966.*

Col. 2–4: ILO, *Yearbook of Labor Statistics.*

Col. 6–8: United Nations, *Statistical Yearbook.*

INDEX